THE WAY
IT WAS
in the WEST

THE WAY IT WAS

in the WEST

Clarence P. Hornung

SMITHMARK

Copyright © 1978 by Abbeville Press

This edition published in 1992 by SMITHMARK Publishers, Inc.
16 East 32nd Street, New York, NY 10016

Printed by special arrangement with
William S. Konecky Associates, Inc.

SMITHMARK books are available for bulk purchase for
sales promotion and premium use. For details write
or telephone the Manager of Special Sales, SMITHMARK
Publishers, Inc., 16 East 32nd Street, New York, NY 10016.
(212) 532-6600.

ISBN 0-8317-9356-2

Printed in the United States of America

CONTENTS

THE WEST

Over Plains & Prairies
... Ever Westward

OVERLAND MAIL COACH . . .
ATCHISON . . . DENVER CITY . . .
THE FIRST SPIKE . . .CROSSING
THE PLAINS . . . CAMP AT NIGHT
. . . PILGRIMS ON THE PLAINS . . .
COMPLETION OF THE UNION
PACIFIC RAILROAD . . . .PROMONTORY
POINT . . . DENVER AND RIO GRANDE
RAILROAD . . . CENTRAL PACIFIC
RAILROAD . . . TEN MILE CANYON . . .
GIANT'S GAP . . . AMERICAN RIVER . . .
DONNER LAKE . . . JOINING OF THE RAILS
. . . EN ROUTE BY RAIL . . . SCENES
ON AN IMMIGRANT TRAIN . . . AT
THE RAILROAD STATION . . . RED
RIVER . . . FARGO . . . CROW VILLAGE
CORN FARMING . . . CATTLE, ABILENE
. . . TEXAS SHEEP . . . THE ROUND-UP
COWBOYS ON THE PLAINS . . . BUFFALO
BULLS . . . HORSE AUCTION . . . CATTLE
COUNTRY . . . PRAIRIE FARM SKETCHES

Over Plains & Prairies
... Ever Westward

A TEXAN PONY

EVER SINCE THE EARLY YEARS OF THE nineteenth century, explorers had been venturing out beyond the Mississippi into the region now called the Great Plains. Their reports were not often favorable. Zebulon Pike, who traveled into the plains seeking the source of the Mississippi, declared the region to be "incapable of cultivation"; and Major Stephen H. Long, who followed the Platte River into Nebraska, gave the region a name it would bear for much of the century, "The Great American Desert."

Exploration by the white man began only in the early nineteenth century, with the appearance of French and, later, American fur trappers. As the fur trade grew, mountaineers blazed trails to the West. Jedediah Smith

carved out the Overland Trail and demonstrated that it was possible to cross the mountains with wagons. William Becknell established the Santa Fe trail in 1821. By 1841, the first overland party was bound for California. These early pioneers, however, were entering a land that the federal government had reserved by treaty for the Indians, both for those native to the plains and for those who had been moved from their lands east of the Mississippi. In the 1830s and 1840s Plains Indians signed away much of their land, in return for outright payments in cash or goods, stipends, and guarantees of reserved land elsewhere.

Eventually sales and treaties gave way to bloody confrontation, as diseases brought by whites and the flight of the buffalo, caused by the settlers' frequent overland crossings, made life for the Indians unbearable. By the 1850s Indians began to actively harass white settlers and wagon trains, and the first of many legendary figures of the plains—the Warrior and the Indian Fighter—were born. In 1862, starvation among the Santee Dakotas led to serious warfare; hundreds of settlers were massacred and many towns were destroyed. Retaliation was swift and violent. In 1876, Custer's defeat by the Cheyenne and Sioux at Little Bighorn aroused a national fury. The Indians, decimated and starving and hopelessly outnumbered, faced the final slaughter. In 1881 Sitting Bull finally surrendered; the bloody saga was over.

Violence was everywhere in the Great Plains. The Indian wars raged for fifty years; and settlers fought equally bloody battles among themselves. Cattlemen and farmers fought bitterly over use of the land. Disputes over slavery led to outrageous acts of terrorism, even before the Civil War broke out. "Bleeding Kansas" was a battleground for partisans on both sides, before and during the war. After the war, guerilla action continued as attacks on railroads, stagecoaches, and banks were mounted by such legendary outlaws as Jessie James and the Dalton Boys.

Because the land of the Great Plains, and especially the southern parts of it, had never seemed hospitable to farming, many settlers had turned to grazing. But their great distance from the Eastern markets limited profits. By 1867, however, railroads reached out from St. Louis and across Missouri and Iowa, Kansas and Nebraska. The great cattle drives began. At Abiline, Kansas cattle pens were built along the tracks of the Kansas Pacific Railroad. And up from Texas, along the famous Shawnee and Chisholm trails, tens of thousands of cattle were driven along a route that took as long as forty days to travel. It was a rugged journey. Beset by Indian marauders and cattle rustlers, the men driving the great herds carved out their own legend in the harsh plains. By 1871 more than six hundred thousand head of cattle were moving yearly through Abiline. Elsewhere in the plains, the Sante Fe, Union Pacific, and Northern Pacific established other centers. These centers became the first cities of the Plains: Abiline, Wichita, Great Bend, Ellsworth, and Dodge City in Kansas; Ogallala in Nebraska; and Bismark in North Dakota.

While cattle herds were driven north and shipped east, another herd was being slaughtered—the buffalo. The Indians were dependent on this great beast for their very existence: they ate its meat and used its hide for clothing and shelter. It was clear that if deprived of the buffalo, the Indian would disappear. It became federal, state, and territorial policy to rid the plains of buffalo. Other pressures to kill the buffalo existed as well. Cattlemen wanted lands for grazing. The railroads wanted to encourage settlement by ranchers and farmers. Sportsmen simply wanted to hunt. So, by the 1870s, the slaughter of the buffalo became epic. Hundreds of thousands were killed every year, and by 1880 very few were left.

As the land was cleared of buffalo and Indians, and as the railroad spanned the continent, the population of the Great Plains soared. The number of farms doubled. Towns grew, and grew rowdier. Dodge City, prospering first from outfitting buffalo hunters and then from the railroads, became known as "Hell on the Plains," and its Front Street, Alhambra Saloon, Dodge City Opera, and Boot Hill became legends; as did its lawmen, Wyatt Earp and Bat and Jim Masterson.

There were many ways through the West: the Overland and Santa Fe and Chisholm and Shawnee trails; the Union Pacific, Northern Pacific, and the Santa Fe railroads; but the grandest, the busiest, was the Big Muddy—the "Wide Missouri." Long before the trails were blazed and the tracks laid, this river and its branches were moving men toward and through the West. The Missouri travels a course almost twenty-five hundred miles long, and with its branches it touches six of the seven plains states. A mighty and brutal river, it carries loam, marl, gravel, and sand. Floating islands of debris, and sandbars, and shifting currents make travel treacherous. Spring flooding and sudden, swift changes in its own bed maroon and often destroy whole towns. The Missouri could never be wholly tamed, but for some forty years, beginning in the 1840s, steamboats traveled its waters in a golden age of river commerce.

The Missouri was and is still a great travelway, but it has also nourished the Great Plains. The river itself and its tributaries flow through one of the most fertile areas on earth —the endless corn fields of Iowa and the wheat fields of Kansas, Nebraska, and North Dakota. To the farmers and the cattlemen who fought the river, the elements, the Indians, the outlaws, and each other, this land, "incapable of cultivation," has yielded an endless bounty.

"Westward the course of the empire takes its way"—the slogan stresses the need for news between the distant West and the rest of the nation, after the discovery of gold in California . . .

Prior to the discovery of gold in California there was no regular line of communication between the eastern United States and its Pacific territory. The steamers that sailed around the Horn constituted a very slow and intermittent contact. As a result of being cut off from the centers of trade and government Californians stirred up a great deal of agitation during the 40's and 50's. The governor and legislature pushed a vigorous program, not only for the building of railroads but for the regular schedule of an overland mail service to supplement the semi-monthly mails that arrived by slow boat. A monster petition bearing 75,000 signatures was sent to Washington in 1856, resulting in Congress' appropriation of $550,000 for three wagon roads. Finally, in 1857 a bill was passed authorizing a line "from such point on the Mississippi River as the contractors may select, to San Francisco in the State of California, for six years—cost not to exceed $300,000 per annum for a semi-monthly service, $450,000 for weekly and $600,000 for a semi-weekly service." The Post Office advertised for bids as prescribed and received nine, the successful bidders John Butterfield, William Fargo and others, all experienced in the express business. Postmaster Brown, from Tennessee, insisted upon a southerly route in spite of angry protests from many sections of the north. The final route formed a roundabout semi-circle from St. Louis, via El Paso and Fort Yuma, a distance of 2800 miles, favored over the northerly route via Salt Lake City.

CLARENCE P. HORNUNG

Wheels Across America,

1959

BUTTERFIELD'S OVERLAND MAIL, FROM SAN FRANCISCO FOR THE EAST

OVERLAND MAIL COACH LEAVING ATCHISON, KANSAS

. . . resulting, in 1858, in the inauguration of the overland stagecoach lines for delivery of mail, express matter, and passenger service—two years before the pony express

. . . On September 16, 1857, service was inaugurated on both east and western terminals, after a year of energetic preparations during which hundreds of way stations were built, wells sunk for water, teams procured and drivers trained. The first trips carrying only mail and papers, arrived ahead of the 25 day schedule. Both in St. Louis and San Francisco, the opening of the line was the occasion of much rejoicing—long parades, brass bands, salutes and unbridled jubilation were the order of the day. The famous Concord coaches, sturdily built spring wagons, stood up remarkably well under the continuous strain of the long journey. At first they carried few passengers but later on they were enlarged to accommodate up to nine inside and as many who dared cling to the outside seats were carried on top. Teams of four to six mustangs—"wild as deer"—sped the coaches over the usual 10 to 15 miles between stations. The fare from St. Louis was $100 to the east, $200 for the western trip, and meals were extra.

CLARENCE P. HORNUNG
Wheels Across America,
1959

OVERLAND COACH OFFICE, DENVER, COLORADO

EASTERN TERMINUS OF THE
OVERLAND ROUTE, ATCHISON

DRIVING THE FIRST SPIKE, ON
THE ATCHISON AND PIKE'S PEAK R.R.

6

"It is our manifest destiny to overspread and possess the whole of the continent which Providence has given us for the great experiment of liberty," said John O'Sullivan, in 1845

. . . our manifest destiny is to overspread and to possess the whole of the continent which Providence has given us for the development of the great experiment of liberty and federated self-government entrusted to us.

JOHN LOUIS O'SULLIVAN
New York Morning News,
December 27, 1845

PILGRIMS ON THE PLAINS

Not to-day, nor to-morrow, but this government is to last, I trust, forever; we may at least hope it will endure until the wave of population, cultivation, and intelligence shall have washed the Rocky Mountains and mingled with the Pacific. And may we not also hope that the day will arrive when the improvements and comforts to social life shall spread over the vast area of the continent? . . . It is a peculiar delight to me to look forward to the proud and happy period, distant as it may be, when circulation and association between the Atlantic and Pacific and the Mexican Gulf shall be as free and perfect as they are at this moment in England or in any other country of the globe.

HENRY CLAY
Speech of January 31, 1824

THE OLD BONE MAN OF THE PLAINS

The westward way pointed far beyond the reaches of the Mississippi—with crossings by long caravans of "prairie schooners"—handcart brigades of the Mormons, or by shank's mare

ARMY TRAIN CROSSING THE PLAINS

The *untransacted* destiny of the American people is to subdue the continent—to rush over this vast field to the Pacific Ocean—to animate the many hundreds of millions of its people, to cheer them upward . . . . to agitate these herculean masses—to establish a new order in human affairs . . . to regenerate the superannuated nations—to stir up the sleep of a hundred centuries—to teach old nations a new civilization—to confirm the destiny of the human race—to carry the career of mankind to its culminating point—to perfect science—to emblazon history with the conquest of peace—to shed a new and resplendent glory upon mankind—to unite the world in one social family.

WILLIAM GILPIN
A published letter, 1846

AROUND THE CAMPFIRE AT NIGHT

Journalists like John Soule and Horace Greeley, sensing the surging expansionist movement urged: "Go west, young man, and grow up with the country." The pressure of newspaper publicity . . .

On the morning of May 10, 1869, Hon. Leland Stanford, Governor of California and President of the Central Pacific, accompanied by Messrs. Huntington, Hopkins Crocker and trainloads of California's distinguished citizens, arrived from the west. During the forenoon Vice President T. C. Durant and Directors John R. Duff and Sidney Dillon and Consulting Engineer Silas A. Seymour of the Union Pacific, with other prominent men, including a delegation of Mormons from Salt Lake City, came in on a train from the east. The National Government was represented by a detachment of "regulars" from Fort Douglass, Utah, accompanied by a band, and 600 others, including Chinese, Mexicans, Indians, half-breeds, negroes and laborers, suggesting an air of cosmopolitanism, all gathered around the open space where the tracks were to be joined. The Chinese laid the rails from the west end, and the Irish laborers laid them from the east end, until they met and joined.

GREENVILLE M. DODGE

How We Built the Union Pacific Railway, 1869

What was it the Engines said,
Pilots touching, head to head
Facing on a single track,
Half a world behind each back?

You brag of the East! You do?
Why, I bring the East to you!
All the Orient, all Cathay,
Find through me the shortest way;
And the sun you follow here
Rises in my hemisphere!

THE MEETING OF THE RAILS, PROMONTORY POINT, UTAH

THE GREAT LOOP OF THE DENVER AND RIO GRANDE R.R.

Colloquy by
BRET HARTE

. . . led to the Pacific Railroad Act of 1862—signed by President Lincoln during the Civil War crisis—to help speed army trains and forge a union of East and West

CENTRAL PACIFIC R.R., NEAR THE AMERICAN RIVER   DONNER LAKE

Each day taught us lessons by which we profited for the next, and our advances and improvements in the art of railway construction were marked by the progress of the work, forty miles of track having been laid in 1865, 260 in 1866, 240 in 1867, including the ascent to the summit of the Rocky mountains, at an elevation of 8235 feet above the ocean; and during 1868 and to May 10, 1869, 555 miles all exclusive of side and temporary tracks, of which over 180 miles were built in addition. The first grading was done in the autumn of 1864, and the first rail laid in July, 1865. When you look back to the beginning at the Missouri river, with no railroad communication from the east, and 500 miles of the country in advance without timber, fuel or any material whatever from which to build or maintain a road, except the sand for the bare roadbed itself with everything to be transported, and that by teams or at best by steamboats, for hundreds and thousands of miles; everything to be created, with labor scarce and high, you can all look back upon the work with satisfaction and ask, under such circumstances, could we have done more or better? The country is evidently satisfied that you accomplish wonders and have achieved a work that will be a monument to your energy, your ability, and to your devotion to the enterprise through all its gloomy as well as its bright periods; for it is notorious that, notwithstanding the aid of the Government, there was so little faith in the enterprise that its dark days—when your private fortunes and your all was staked on the success of the project—far exceeded those of sunshine, faith and confidence.

GREENVILLE M. DODGE
*How We Built the Union
Pacific Railway, 1869*

CENTRAL PACIFIC R.R., TEN-MILE CANYON, NEVADA

LABORERS, CENTRAL PACIFIC R.R.   GIANT'S GAP, CENTRAL PACIFIC R.R.

As Appomattox had reunited the North and South—
Promontary Point had joined the East and West—
a continent united—"one and indivisible"

I remember that the parties going to Salt Lake crossed the Wasatch Mountain on sledges and that the snow covered the tops of the telegraph poles. We all knew and appreciated that the task we had laid out would require the greatest energy on the part of all hands. About April 1st, therefore, I went on to the plains myself and started our construction forces, remaining the whole summer between Laramie and the Humboldt Mountains. I was surprised at the rapidity with which the work was carried forward. Winter caught us in the Wasatch Mountains, but we kept on grading our road and laying our track in the snow and ice, at a tremendous cost. I estimated for the company that the extra cost of thus forcing the work during that summer and winter was over ten million dollars, but the instructions I received were to go on, no matter what the cost. Spring found us with the track to Ogden, and by May 1st we had reached Promontory, five hundred and thirty-four miles west of our starting point twelve months before. Work on our line was opened to Humboldt Wells, making in the year a grading of seven hundred and fifty-four miles of line.

GREENVILLE M. DODGE

How We Built the Union
Pacific Railway, 1869

THE LINKING OF EAST AND WEST . . . COMPLETION OF THE RAILS, MAY 10, 1869

The Golden Spike ceremony symbolizing the spanning of the continent, in 1869, brought the Union Pacific eastward, and the Central Pacific westward to join rails

The great Pacific railway,
  For California hail!
Bring on the locomotive,
  Lay down the iron rail;
Across the rolling prairies
  By steam we're bound
  to go,
The railroad cars are
  coming, humming
  Through New Mexico,
The railroad cars are
  coming, humming
  Through New Mexico.

The little dogs in dog-town
  Will wag each little tail;
They'll think that
  something's coming
  A-riding on a rail.
The rattle-snake will show
  its fangs,
  The owl tu-whit,
  tu-who,
The railroad cars are
  coming, humming
  Through New Mexico,
The railroad cars are
  coming, humming
  Through New Mexico.

CARL SANDBURG

*The Railroad Cars
Are Coming*

*In 1882, the Southern Pacific in the Southwest extended its lines,
forming a through passage from New Orleans to San Francisco.
In 1883, the Northwest was joined from St. Paul to Portland*

Immigrants reached the United States in extraordinary numbers during the early and mid '80's. In the fiscal year ending June 30, 1882, nearly 800,000 persons had arrived, about 35 percent of whom were English-speaking. England, Ireland, Scotland sent nearly 180,000; Canada over 98,000. Next in number were the Germans—nearly a quarter of a million. Sweden was represented with about 64,000; Norway with over 29,000; the Celestial Kingdom sent nearly 40,000; Italy over 32,000. All were said to be of excellent average character and many arrived, as *Harper's Weekly,* February 10, 1883, said: "with well-defined plans as to their places of destination, and for the most part provided with the railway tickets for their journey inland." Agents for the various railroads immediately took charge of these groups, placing the women and children—"with their natural protectors, if they have any"—in separate cars; keeping the "rougher persons" by themselves. A contemporary account says:

A BREAKDOWN ON THE ROAD

THE "MODERN SHIP OF THE PLAINS"

As railroads crisscrossed the nation in a network of trunk lines and branches to serve the ever wider areas, thousands of immigrants and travelers crossed the plains

A Stop on the Road
"Get on Board there!"

W·A·Rogers.

Immigrant Inspection Service.

The Youngsters.

ABOARD AN IMMIGRANT TRAIN—WESTWARD BOUND

"At the start the cars are rude but cleanly. Plenty of fresh water is supplied. Some effort is made, too, to keep the air fresh and the car decent, but this is very difficult. . . . Pipes are lighted; meals are spread in which sausage, garlic and sauerkraut form prominent elements, and the mingled odors combine with the smoke of cheap tobacco to render the cars insupportable . . . . When the train stops, laden with its miscellaneous freight, the adults are glad to alight; the children rush eagerly about gathering the oddest mementoes of their journey. Occasionally a kitten is captured to the delight of the whole carload . . . . It is petted, fed, put to sleep in dinner pails, and rarely abused." Before arrival at Chicago —which was the main point of distribution —sanitary inspectors came aboard the emigrant trains, conducting a very thorough inspection, principally with reference to smallpox. These men were under the direction of the National Board of Health. They inquired as to the general condition of the immigrants, then as to the date of vaccination, and its effectiveness. At Castle Garden, in New York—between the arrival of the steamship and the evening departure of the Westbound trains—the colorful array of foreign costumes was described in *Frank Leslie's Illustrated Newspaper,* May 1, 1880: "The quaint costumes of Danish and German villages, the rich colors of Connemara cloaks, the hues of the beribboned lassies from many climes, blend in glowing contrasts, while the immigrants sit or sprawl in indolent nonchalance in the Castle Garden rotunda."

CLARENCE P. HORNUNG
Wheels Across America, 1959

The railroads bound distant and diverse regions together—travel increased, building towns and creating new markets, exerting a unifying influence on our national life

Everywhere, the early railways acted like magnets; they drew people—idlers and busy alike—to the depot. From sleepy towns to quick-paced cities, the railway station could usually be counted on as the place where interesting things would be happening. The steam locomotives were exciting enough; and the welcomes to people arriving—the farewells to those departing—on a journey, were as good as a gossip column to keep one informed on the town's doings. Judge Gillis who, in 1835, took his first train ride behind the *"DeWitt Clinton,"* left additional notes on his experience. "The incidents off the train were quite as striking as those on the train; everybody, together with his wife and all his children, came from a distance with all kinds of conveyances, and being as ignorant of what was coming as their horses, drove as near as they could get, only looking for the best position to get a view of the train. As it approached, the horses took fright and wheeled, upsetting buggies, carriages, and wagons . . . and it is not now positively known in some of them have stopped yet." Now, around the seventies, the horses were less excitable, but the depot as a focus of local interest held an undiminished charm . . .

THE WAITING ROOM AT A COUNTRY DEPOT

THE RUSH FOR THE COUNTRY

Every town—even tiny hamlets on branch spurs—had its railroad depot, a new social center where arrivals and departures crammed waiting rooms with people and baggage

TRIALS OF THE BAGGAGE MASTER

. . .The old, bulging "balloon" or "diamond" shaped smokestacks were still in use, on locomotives during the Reconstruction era. Never designed for ornament, they served the utilitarian purpose of catching sparks and cinders from the wood-burning engines. When coal succeeded the use of wood as fuel, smokestacks were modified into a straight and narrow shape. Train conductors wore ordinary clothes and their attempts to collect fares were often resented by inexperienced travelers. A suspicion-ridden Senator from the West, on his first train journey, punched the conductor who tried to take his ticket. The Senator was determined not to be cheated by a railway "sharper." Soon, train employees were required to wear uniforms.

CLARENCE P. HORNUNG
Wheels Across America, 1959

HOME FOR THE HOLIDAYS

In the northern plains regions of the Dakota and Minnesota Territories—along the headwaters of the Mississippi, Missouri, Red, Platte, and Yellowstone rivers . . .

Out where the hand-clasp's a little stronger,
Out where the smile dwells a little longer,
   That's where the West begins;
Out where the sun is a little brighter,
Where the snows that fall are a trifle whiter,
Where the bonds of home are a wee bit tighter,
   That's where the West begins.

Out where the skies are a little bluer,
Out where friendship's a little truer,
   That's where the West begins;
Out where a fresher breeze is blowing,
Where there's laughter in every streamlet flowing,
Where there's more of reaping and less of sowing,
   That's where the West begins.

Out where the world is in the making,
Where fewer hearts in despair are aching,
   That's where the West begins;
Where there's more of singing and less of sighing,
Where there's more of giving and less of buying,
And a man makes friends without half trying—
   That's where the West begins.

ARTHUR CHAPMAN
Out Where the West Begins, 1911

RED RIVER, DAKOTA

THE HEAD OF NAVIGATION, RED RIVER, FARGO, DAKOTA

. . . fur traders and homesteaders learned to co-exist with natives of many tribes—the Assiniboin, Sioux, Mandan, Blackfeet, Dakota, Crow, and Cheyennes

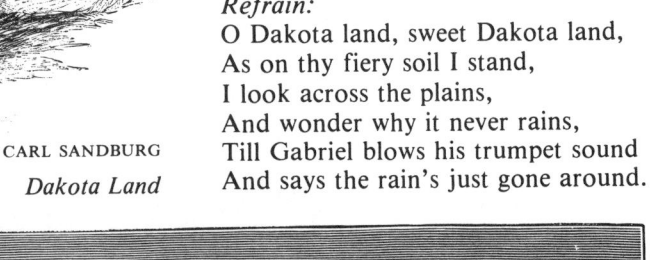

LITTLE CROW VILLAGE, ON THE MISSISSIPPI

We've reached land of desert sweet,
Where nothing grows for man to eat,
The wind it blows with feverish heat
Across the plains so hard to beat.

We've reached the land of hills and
    stones
Where all is strewn with buffalo bones.
O buffalo bones, bleached buffalo
    bones,
I seem to hear your sighs and moans.

We have no wheat, we have no oats,
We have no corn to feed out shoats;
Our chickens are so very poor
They beg for crumbs outside the door.

Refrain:
O Dakota land, sweet Dakota land,
As on thy fiery soil I stand,
I look across the plains,
And wonder why it never rains,
Till Gabriel blows his trumpet sound
And says the rain's just gone around.

CARL SANDBURG
Dakota Land

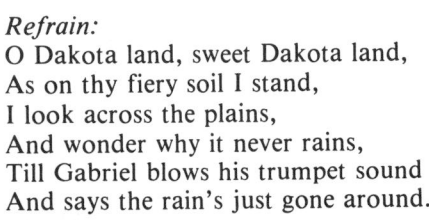

INDIAN VILLAGE, DAKOTA

Throughout the Midwest, limitless prairie lands proved ideal for growing wheat, grains, and especially corn in Illinois, Indiana, Iowa, Kansas, and Missouri . . .

Corn is the greatest of all American crops; it grows in every state and in both value and production it outranks wheat, oats, rice, and rye combined. Glance at a Department of Agriculture map, showing the total American acreage of corn, with a black dot for every thousand acres. Parts of the map look like the ink blot tests used in psychiatry. The central puddle is Iowa—Iowa is so solid with black that you cannot see where the state begins or ends. Then smears and blobs drip over into adjacent areas, particularly in Nebraska and Illinois. Corn is everything in Iowa; it is eggs, milk, breakfast cereals, cattle, meal, chemicals, syrup, starch, liquor, and pork. But the chief thing to know about it is that it is not corn. It is hogs. The "corn-hog ratio," which can be worked out by a child on a blackboard, dominates corn as the formula $E = mc^2$ dominates the production of atomic energy. Corn grows on 11 million acres in Iowa, but only an infinitesimal fraction of these produce corn to be eaten as corn—in the shape of corn on the cob, popcorn or sweet corn. The enormous preponderance of production goes to "field corn," viz., corn fed to animals—chiefly hogs. Corn is not a corn problem at all. It is a pork problem and to some extent a beef and poultry problem.

JOHN GUNTHER
Inside U.S.A., 1937

PLANTING CORN.

FARM GANG.

A

BREAK

SUNDAY IN "BURR OAK" GROVE.

A LARGE FARM IN THE WEST . . .

. . . the corn harvest, as autumn touched the long leaves with brown, called for large work gangs and teams of powerful oxen, used for heavy hauling in all seasons

CULTIVATING CORN.

HEDGE GANG.

RIE.

M. L. SULLIVANT AND HIS CAPTAINS AT EVENING.

THE GROWING, CULTIVATION, AND PICKING OF A CORN HARVEST, "BURR OAK" FARM, ILLINOIS

The westward movement recovered momentum after the hard times of 1837-41. New Englanders, who a generation before had settled the interior of New York and Ohio, now pressed into the smaller prairies of Indiana and Illinois, where the tough sod taxed their strength but repaid it with bountiful crops of grain; where shoulder-high prairie grass afforded rich pasturage for cattle, and groves of buckeye, oak, walnut, and hickory furnished wood and timber. A favorite objective for Yankee settlement was southern Michigan, a rolling country of "oak openings," where stately trees stood well spaced as in a park. Others were hewing farms from the forests of southern Wisconsin, and venturing across the Mississippi into land vacated by Black Hawk's warriors—to Minnesota.

SAMUEL ELIOT MORISON
The Oxford History of the American People, 1965

I must soon quit the scene, but you may live to see our country flourish; as it will amazingly and rapidly after the war is over; like a field of young Indian corn, which long fair weather and sunshine had enfeebled and discolored, and which in that weak state, by a sudden gust of violent wind, hail, and rain, seemed to be threatened with absolute destruction; yet the storm being past, it recovers fresh verdure, shoots up with double vigor, and delights the eye not of its owners only, but of every observing traveler.

BENJAMIN FRANKLIN
Letter to Washington, March 5, 1780

*High drama on the range was the daily chore of the rancher—
protecting the herds from rustlers, guiding half-wild longhorns
or sheep on long drives to market, via rails to the north*

There was commotion in Roaring Camp. It could not have been a fight, for in 1850 that was not novel enough to have called together the entire settlement. The ditches and claims were not only deserted, but "Tuttle's grocery" had contributed its gamblers, who, it will be remembered, calmly continued their game the day that French Pete and Kanaka Joe shot each other to death over the bar in the front room. The whole camp was collected before a rude cabin on the outer edge of the clearing. Conversation was carried on in a low tone, but the name of a woman was frequently repeated. It was a name familiar enough in the camp,—"Cherokee Sal." Perhaps the less said of her the better. She was a coarse and, it is to be feared, a very sinful woman. But at that time she was the only woman in Roaring Camp, and was just then lying in sore extremity, when she most needed the ministration of her own sex. Dissolute, abandoned, and irreclaimable, she was yet suffering a martyrdom hard enough to bear even when veiled by sympathizing womanhood, but now terrible in her loneliness. The primal curse had come to her in that original isolation which must have made the punishment of the first transgression so dreadful.

BRET HARTE

The Luck of the Roaring Camp, 1868

CATTLE DRIFTING ON THE RANGE

HERDING CATTLE INTO CHUTE

The cattle drove emerged as one of the most picturesque episodes enacted on the wide empire of grassland—the Great Plains of the West

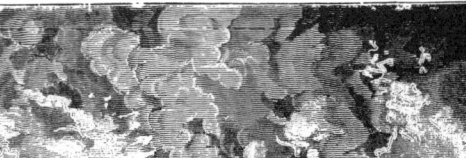

ROUND-UP TIME

At last, after days of excitement and danger and after months of weary, monotonous toil, the chosen ground is reached and the final camp pitched. The footsore animals are turned loose to shift for themselves, outlying camps of two or three men each being established to hem them in. Meanwhile the primitive ranch-house, out-buildings, and corrals are built, the unhewn cottonwood logs being chinked with moss and mud, while the roofs are of branches covered with dirt, spades and axes being the only tools needed for the work. Bunks, chairs, and tables are all home-made, and as rough as the houses they are in. The supplies of coarse, rude food are carried perhaps two or three hundred miles from the nearest town, either in the ranch-wagons or else by some regular freighting outfit, the huge canvas-topped prairie schooners of which are each drawn by several yoke of oxen, or perhaps by six or eight mules.

THEODORE ROOSEVELT
Ranch Life and the Hunting—Trail, 1902

HERDERS DRIVING SHEEP BEFORE A PRAIRIE FIRE

The rugged life of the cowboy on the range, depicted in its varied phases and experiences by the great Western illustrator Frederick Remington, brought intimate details . . .

The round-up is the harvest of the range. Therefore it is natural that its customs should offer more of interest than those of any other part of the year. It were matter of course, also, that features so singular and stirring in their intense action as those of the cowman's harvest should be known and blazoned about for the knowledge of those living elsewhere than upon the cattle fields. Writers and artists have seized upon this phase of the cattle man's life, and given it so wide a showing that the public might well have at least a general idea of the subject. Yet perhaps this general idea would be a more partial and less accurate notion than is deserved by the complicated and varied business system of the cattle harvest. If we would have a just idea of the life and character of the man who makes the round-up, we should approach the subject rather with a wish to find its fundamental principles than a desire to see its superficial pictures . . .

MIDDAY MEAL

BUFFALO BULLS PROTECTING A HERD FROM WOLVES

. . . of cowpunching, cattle droving, round-ups,
and rodeos to thousands of readers across the nation
—through the pages of the weekly and monthly journals

. . . The system of the round-up, while it retains the same general features over the whole of the cow country, and has done so for years, is none the less subject to considerable local modifications, and it has in many respects changed with the years as other customs of the industry have changed; for not even the ancient and enduring calling of the cowman could be free from the law of progress. The Western traveller who first saw a round-up twenty years ago would not be in position to describe one of to-day. Sectional differences make still other changes which should be regarded. Yet all these round-ups, of the past and of the present, of the North and of the South, ground themselves upon a common principle—namely, upon that desire for absolute justice which has been earlier mentioned as a distinguishing trait of the cowman and the trade he follows.

EMERSON HOUGH
The Story of the Cowboy, 1897

CHUCK-WAGON ON "ROUND-UP"

ARIZONA COWBOYS WARNED BY A SCOUT

*The empire of the longhorn—of cattleman and nester,
of homesteaders and ranchers, miles of barbed-wire fencing to
keep cattle in and rustlers out—this was the cow kingdom . . .*

When the glow of fading sunlight,
  Gives way to gath'ring dark,
A lone campfire's glowing embers,
  Release gold-gleaming sparks;
A man sits in the deep shadows,
  In a posture of rest—
He's a man of rugged ranges,
  Man of the open West.

He's ridden atop the springtime,
  He's scorched in summer heat;
He has known Old Winter's
    scourging,
  By frozen hands and feet,
Without a sign of a whimper,
  He long has faced the test;
He's a true son of the ranges,
  Man of the open West.

A face that is tan and freckled,
  Stubby beard on his chin;
A chest that is broad and muscled,
  And heart that's true within;
His legs are strong and sturdy built,
  Bowed a bit at the best,
This son of the rugged ranges—
  Man of the open West.

ARTHUR W. MONROE
The Man of the Open West

IN WITH THE HORSE HERD

AN EXPLORING OUTFIT

A BUCKING BRONCO

. . . where cowhands fought Indians and poachers, herdmen drove cattle on the long, long trails—the Chisholm Trail, the Western Trail, and the Shawnee Trail from lower Texas

CUTTING OUT A STEER

Night on the prairies,
The supper is over, the fire on the ground burns low,
The wearied emigrants sleep, wrapt in their blankets;
I walk by myself—I stand and look at the stars, which
    I think now I never realized before.

Now I absorb immortality and peace,
I admire death and test propositions.

How plenteous! how spiritual! how resumé!
The same old man and soul—the same old aspirations,
    and the same content.

I was thinking the day most splendid till I saw what the
    not-day exhibited,
I was thinking this globe enough till there sprang out so
    noiseless around me myriads of other globes.

Now while the great thoughts of space and eternity fill me
    I will measure myself by them,
And now touch'd with the lives of other globes arrived
    as far along as those of the earth,
Or waiting to arrive, or pass'd on farther than those of the
    earth,
I henceforth no more ignore them than I ignore my own life,
Or the lives of the earth arrived as far as mine, or
    waiting to arrive.

WALT WHITMAN
Night on the Prairies

AN EPISODE IN THE OPENING UP OF A CATTLE COUNTRY

The prairie was a boundless farmland—its rich soil of sand and gravel, clay and loam deposited by the broad glacier that overspread the continent—had to be tamed and worked from dawn to dusk

As I look back over my life on that Iowa farm the song of the reaper fills large place in my mind. We were all worshipers of wheat in those days. The men thought and talked of little else between seeding and harvest, and you will not wonder at this if you have known and bowed before such abundance as we then enjoyed. Deep as the breast of a man, wide as the sea, heavy-headed, supple-stocked, many-voiced, full of multitudinous, secret, whispered coloquies—a meeting place of winds and of sunlight—our fields ran to the world's end. We trembled when the storm lay hard upon the wheat, we exulted as the lilac shadows of noonday drifted over it! We went out into it at noon when all was still—so still we could hear the pulse of the transforming sap as it crept from cool root to swaying plume. We stood before it at evening when the setting sun flooded it with crimson, the bearded heads lazily swirling under the wings of the wind, the mousing hawk dipping into its green deeps like the eagle into the sea, and our hearts expanded with the beauty and the mystery of it—and back of all this was the knowledge that its abundance meant a new carriage, an addition to the house, or a new suit of clothes. Haying was over, and day by day we boys watched with deepening interest while the hot sun transformed the juices of the soil into those stately stalks. I loved to go out into the fairy forest of it, and lying there, silent in its swaying deeps, hear the wild chickens peep and the wind sing its subtle song over our heads.

HAMLIN GARLAND

A Son of the Middle Border,

1917

1. Turf House.—2. Claim Shanty.—3. Hay Stable.—4. Interior of Mud House.—5. Carrying Grain to Market.—6. Log and Mud House.—7. Breaking. 8. Cross Ploughing.—9. Seeding.—10. Dragging.—11. Spring Work Finished—Waiting for the Harvest.—12. Cutting.—13. Binding.—14. Loading.—15. Threshing.—16. Bagging the Grain.—17. The Grain Elevator.

SCENES ON A PRAIRIE FARM, MINNESOTA

From Yellowstone...
through the Rockies...
to the Sierras

THE LITTLE COLORADO . . . THE
YELLOWSTONE . . . YELLOWSTONE LAKE
. . . TOWER FALLS . . . THE LOWER FALLS
. . . HOT SPRINGS . . . GIANT GEYSER . . .
GREEN RIVER, BUTTES . . . ECHO CANYON
WEBER RIVER . . . BAD LANDS . . . SALT
LAKE CITY . . . MORMONS CROSSING PLAINS
. . . MORMON TEMPLE . . . THE TABERNACLE . . .
LARAMIE PLAINS . . . CHURCH BUTTE . . .
RED BUTTES . . . CHICAGO LAKE . . . PIKES
PEAK . . . GARDEN OF THE GODS . . . MOUNTAIN
OF THE HOLY CROSS . . . SILVER LAKE . . .
LEADVILLE, COLORADO . . . PARIS, TEXAS
. . . COLORADO IRRIGATION . . . BLACK
CANYONS . . . UTE RESERVATION . . . INGRAM
FALLS . . . MARSHALL BASIN . . . GRAND CANYON
. . . KANAB CANYON . . . INNER GORGE . . .
DEVIL'S GATE . . . DONNER LAKE . . . SAN
JOAQUIN RIVER . . . LAKE TAHOE . . .SUMMIT
OF THE SIERRAS . . . MINING CAMP LIFE,
COLORADO

From Yellowstone...
through the Rockies...
to the Sierras

AT THE MOUTH OF THE LITTLE COLORADO

FOR OVER A CENTURY AFTER ITS founding, America's story lay in its great move west. Down the Ohio, over the Appalachians, across the Mississippi, into the plains. With each succeeding decade it seemed that existing borders had grown too confining, and neither rivers, nor mountains, nor Indians, nor the untold hardships of a new, unbroken land could impede the progress west. James Clyman, wagon guide, wrote in 1846, "All ages and sects are found to undertake this long, tedious and even dangerous Journy, for some unknown object never to be realized even by the most fortunate. And why? Because the human mind can never be satisfied, never at rest, always on the stretch for something new."

Almost immediately after the Louisiana Pur-chase, Thomas Jefferson decided to discover what actually lay within and beyond the vast territory just acquired. Captain Meriwether Lewis and Lieutenant William Clark left St. Louis in 1804, under orders from the president to explore the territory, discover its western boundary, and then move on to the Pacific. By way of the Missouri River, through the Dakotas and Montana, and on to the Columbia River watershed in Idaho and Washington—guided through much of the journey by Sacajawea, their Shoshone guide—Lewis and Clark reached the Pacific in the fall of 1805. By the time they returned, they had covered over six thousand miles. At about the same time, the U.S. Army dispatched Lieutenant Zebulon Pike and a large party to explore the central Mountain West. Pike traveled past the

Colorado mountain that would eventually bear his name—Pikes Peak—almost to the source of the Arkansas River in the high Rockies. These expeditions provided the first sure knowledge that the Rockies really did exist, and they charted the western boundary of the Louisiana Territory—the Continental Divide.

More intimate topographical knowledge would be provided by the fur trappers, who began to enter the Rocky Mountains in the years following 1812. In 1824 trappers reached the Green River in Wyoming by crossing the south end of the Wind River Range at South Pass. This crossing revealed the only uninterrupted passage through the Central Rockies. It would become, for decades after, the great overland route to the West.

In the 1830s and 1840s the trappers' knowledge became vital, as the "manifest destiny" preached by politicians and journalists helped to encourage migration by thousands of farmers and missionaries. In the 1840s most immigrants—as pioneers were then called— were going into the Oregon Territory, which covered most of what is now Oregon, Washington, and Idaho. They started in Independence, Missouri, following the Oregon Trail to the Northwest, or the California Trail to Sacramento; some headed southwest along the Santa Fe Trail.

The years 1848 and 1849 were crucial for western migration. Great Britain had already ceded the southern portion of the Oregon Territory; in 1848 Spain relinquished Texas, the Mountain West, and California; and in 1849 James Marshall discovered gold in California's American River. Tens of thousands of immigrants flooded into the West. Most of them took the long, tedious journey by prairie schooner through the South Pass. For eleven years the Gold Rush continued, fueled by additional discoveries of gold in the Colorado Rockies and the Comstock Lode in Nevada. In the 1870s and 1880s the silver boom drove miners again into the western mountains. The Civil War did not interrupt the migration west.

In 1847, a group that was hungry, not for gold or fur, but for freedom from religious persecution, entered the West: the followers of the Church of the Latter-day Saints, the Mormons. Led by Brigham Young, they reached Emigration Canyon in Utah in July 1847. They settled in the valley below and found there the freedom to follow the precepts of their church —including the practice of polygamy for which they had been hounded out of the East. Only in 1896, after polygamy had been abandoned by the church, was Utah allowed to enter the Union. By then the Mormons had built a large and thriving community in the great salt desert.

As with all the westward migration that preceded it, the move into the Rockies and beyond entailed the subjugation of the Indians, many of whom were native to the West and many of whom had fled there when their eastern lands were taken from them. Alarmed by the extension of the railroads in the 1860s, forced into starvation by the slaughter of the buffalo, the Indians fought their last battles in the West. From the 1860s to the 1880s battles and massacres occurred from Montana to Arizona. Indian resistance was fierce and it was bloody—but it was also doomed. A destiny more contrived than manifest favored the Europeans.

The Rockies shelter innumerable streams and great forests. Mighty rivers, like the Arkansas and Colorado, have their source in the Rockies' highest reaches. Canyon walls, like those of the Grand Canyon, rise almost a mile high. Gold, silver, and copper are hidden beneath the soil. Its mountains reach over fourteen thousand feet. It was not an easy land to conquer, but by the turn of the century its peaks, its valleys, its streams, and its forests had been charted, and plundered.

In 1878 Major John Wesley Powell published a pamphlet, *Report on the Lands of the Arid Region*, in which for the first time the aridity, altitude, and climate of the Mountain West were described scientifically. He argued for conserving the vast potential of the mountains; and he could already see that this potential was being wasted. By the 1890s droughts, treeless forests, and grassless plains drove others to see what Powell meant. In 1891 the Forest Reserve Act was passed, putting some thirteen million acres into federal reserves to protect the western watershed. Some years later Theodore Roosevelt added almost one hundred fifty million acres of forest, and another eighty million acres of mineral land to the reserves. These were the first attempts to retrieve the land, not from the English, the Spanish, or the Indians, but from the settlers themselves. It seemed once that nothing could stop the move west and nothing could stem the flow of riches from the land so painfully won. But the Mountain West taught Americans the fragile nature of their mighty possession and showed them the limits of what could finally be grasped.

In the heart of the granitic Rockies—in Wyoming's northwest corner—lies the fabulous Yellowstone, a volcanic interlude between the sharp, serrated Grand Tetons to the south . . .

The Yellowstone River has occasion to run through a gorge about eight miles long. To get to the bottom of the gorge it makes two leaps, one of about one hundred and twenty and the other of three hundred feet. I investigated the upper or lesser fall, which is close to the hotel. Up to that time nothing particular happens to the Yellowstone—its banks being only rocky, rather steep, and plentifully adorned with pines. At the falls it comes round a corner, green, solid, ribbed with a little foam, and not more than thirty yards wide. Then it goes over, still green, and rather more solid than before. After a minute or two, you, sitting upon a rock directly above the drop, begin to understand that something has occurred; that the river has jumped between solid cliff walls, and that the gentle froth of water lapping the sides of the gorge below is really the outcome of great waves. I followed with the others round the corner to arrive at the brink of the canyon. We had to climb up a nearly perpendicular ascent to begin with, for the ground rises more than the river drops. Stately pine woods fringe either lip of the gorge, which is the gorge of the Yellowstone. You'll find all about it in the guide books.

RUDYARD KIPLING

American Notes, 1891

THE YELLOWSTONE

. . . Exploiters who followed the explorers have been busy both at home and abroad rooting up, exterminating or merely pushing to the wall species after species in order to make room for themselves and for "useful" products. The variety of nature grows less and less. The monotony of the chain store begins to dominate more and more completely. One must go farther and farther to find a window in which anything not found elsewhere is to be seen. More than a hundred species and subspecies of mammals are known to have disappeared from the face of the earth since the beginning of the Christian era. Along with them have gone perhaps as many birds and an unknown number of humbler creatures. How many plants have suffered extinction has not, so far as I am aware, been even guessed at.

JOSEPH WOOD KRUTCH

Grand Canyon, 1957

COLUMN ROCKS

. . . and the Montana Rockies' Beartooth and Gallatin Range to the north—an area once the center of violent disturbance where volcanos created natural wonders in infinite variety

TOWER FALLS

Tower Creek rises in the high divide between the valleys of the Missouri and Yellowstone, and flows about ten miles through a canyon so deep and gloomy that it has very properly earned the appellation of the Devil's Den. As we gaze from the margin down into the depths below, the little stream, as it rushes foaming over the rocks, seems like a white thread, while on the sides of the gorge the sombre pinnacles rise up like Gothic spires. About two hundred yards above its entrance into the Yellowstone, the stream pours over an abrupt descent of one hundred and fifty-six feet, forming one of the most beautiful and picturesque falls to be found in any country. The Tower Falls are about two hundred and sixty feet above the level of the Yellowstone at the junction, and they are surrounded with pinnacle-like columns, composed of the volcanic breccia, rising fifty feet above the falls, and extending down to the foot, standing like gloomy sentinels or like the gigantic pillars at the entrance of some grand temple. One could almost imagine that the idea of the Gothic style of architecture had been caught from such carvings of nature. Immense boulders of basalt and granite here obstruct the flow of the stream above and below the falls; and although, so far as we can see, the gorge seems to be made up of the volcanic cement, yet we know that, in the loftier mountains, near the source of the stream, true granitic as well as igneous rocks prevail.

O.B. BUNCE

Picturesque America, 1872

YELLOWSTONE LAKE

The Yellowstone begins in the broad rolling highland known as the Absaroka, flowing north—creating the Great Falls, twice Niagara's height—to form the Grand Canyon with the steep, lava-sided walls . . .

From the surface of a rocky plain or table [Yellowstone's Upper Geyser Basin], burst forth columns of water, of various dimensions, projected high in the air, accompanied by loud explosions, and sulphurous vapors, which were highly disagreeable to the smell. . . . The largest of these wonderful fountains, projects a column of boiling water several feet in diameter, to the height of more than one hundred and fifty feet . . . accompanied with a tremendous noise. These explosions and discharges occur at intervals of about two hours . . . . The Indians who were with me, were quite appalled, and could not by any means be induced to approach them . . . .They believed them to be supernatural, and supposed them to be the production of the Evil Spirit. One of them remarked that hell, of which he had heard from the whites, must be in the vicinity.

WARREN ANGUS FERRIS

Life in the Rocky Mountains,
1834

THE LOWER FALLS

. . . a thousand feet deep, which, for vivid and varied colorations and fantastic sculptured carvings, is second only to the glorious Grand Canyon of the Colorado

We drifted on, up that miraculous valley. On either side of us were hills from a thousand or fifteen hundred feet high, wooded from crest to heel. As far as the eye could range forward were columns of steam in the air, misshapen lumps of lime, mist-like preadamite monsters, still pools of turquoise-blue stretches of blue cornflowers, a river that coiled on itself twenty times, pointed boulders of strange colors, and ridges of glaring, staring white. A moon-faced trooper of German extraction—never was park so carefully patrolled—came up to inform us that as yet we had not seen any of the real geysers; that they were all a mile or so up the valley, and tastefully scattered round the hotel in which we would rest for the night. America is a free country, but the citizens look down on the soldier. I had to entertain that trooper. The old lady from Chicago would have none of him; so we loafed alone together, now across half-rotten pine logs sunk in swampy ground, anon over the ringing geyser formation, then pounding through river-sand or brushing knee-deep through long grass.

RUDYARD KIPLING
American Notes, 1891

CLIFFS ON THE YELLOWSTONE

Ancient geologic upheavals fired nature's forces, creating constant restlessness of "bubbling mud, boiling springs, erupting waterspouts, and subterranean fires" . . .

But the most remarkable of all the springs at this point are six or seven of a character differing from any of the rest. The water in them is of a dark blue or ultra-marine hue, but it is wonderfully clear and transparent. Two of these springs are quite large; the remaining five are smaller, their diameters ranging from eight to fifteen feet . . . . The largest two of these springs are irregular in their general outline of nearly an oval shape, the larger of the two being about twenty-five feet wide by forty long, and the smaller about twenty by thirty feet. Six miles above the upper fall we entered upon a region remarkable for the number and variety of its hot springs and craters. The principal spring, and the one that first meets the eye as you approach from the north, is a hot sulphur spring, of oval shape, the water of which is constantly boiling and is thown up to the height of from three to seven feet . . . . This spring is situated at the base of a low mountain and the gentle slope below and around the spring for the distance of two hundred or three hundred feet is covered from a depth of from three to ten inches with the sulphurous deposit from the overflow of the spring. The moistened bed of a dried-up rivulet, leading from the edge of the spring down inside through this deposit, showed us that the spring had but recently been overflowing. Farther along the base of this mountain is a sulphurous cavern . . . out of which the steam is thrown in jets with a sound resembling the puffing of a steam-boat when laboring over a sand-bar, and with as much uniformity and intonation as if emitted by a high-pressure engine. From hundreds of fissures in the adjoining mountain from base to summit, issue hot sulphur vapors, the apertures through which they escape being encased in thick incrustations of sulphur, which in many instances is perfectly pure. There are nearby a number of small sulphur springs, not especially remarkable in appeerence.

NATHANIEL P. LANGFORD
Diary of the Washburn Expedition to the Yellowstone and Firehole Rivers, 1871

HOT SPRINGS

MUD SPRINGS

*. . . but the most spectacular sight is the action of
"Old Faithful"—a geyser which performs its awe-inspiring
eruption with regularity, reaching a height of 250 feet*

THE GIANT GEYSER

Old Faithful geyser, when all is said, must remain the traveler's favorite. It is beautiful and faithful and perfect and very venerable. It is the first to welcome his arrival. It performs a miracle every sixty-five minutes of his stay. It is the last to speed him onward. And it would have performed the same good offices, back there in the small hours of history, for the same traveler's inarticulate ancestors, when they were still swinging from branch to branch,—provided they had had the good sense to swing in his direction. Every evening a search-light on the Inn roof is trained upon one of Old Faithful's performances. One does not forget a scene like that. We were sitting there, perhaps a hundred pilgrims of us, as Old Faithful once more took its famous leap and spread itself out on the breeze. The search-light casually regarded the spectacle, and instantly there came upon the wall of steam and spray a circular rainbow surrounded by an aureole of misty gold. Then the lens was thrown out of focus, and one could distinctly catch the thrill which ran through the crowd as purple, then emerald, then violet overspread the base of that miracle of cloud soaring up through the fiery rain. One could feel the common human heart throb faster as at the climax of some supreme symphony or drama.

ROBERT HAVEN SCHAUFFLER
Romantic America, 1913

Eons ago, deep beneath an inland sea that covered the region, the Rockies slowly pushed their way to the surface, erupting in jagged peaks and vast plateaus . . .

BUTTES, GREEN RIVER

Near the head of Echo Canyon stands Castle Rock, one of the noblest of the great natural landmarks that are passed in all the route—a vast and ragged pile of massive stone, fantastically cut, by all those mighty forces that toil through the centuries, into the very semblance of a mountain-fortress. A cavernous opening simulates a giant door of entrance between its rounded and overhanging towers; the jagged points above are like the ruins of battlements left bristling and torn after combats of Titans; the huge layers of its worn sides seem to have been builded by skilful hands; and the great rounded foundations, from which the sandy soil has been swept away, would appear rooted in the very central earth. It surmounts a lofty, steep-sided eminence, and frowns down with an awesome strength and quiet on the lonely valley below it.

All Sunday and Monday we travelled through these sad mountains, or over the main ridge of the Rockies, which is a fair match to them for misery of aspect. Hour after hour it was the same unhomely and unkindly world about our onward path; tumbled boulders, cliffs that drearily imitate the shape of monuments and fortifications—how drearily, how tamely, none can tell who has not seen them; not a tree, not a patch of sward, not one shapely or commanding mountain form; sage-brush, eternal sage-brush; over all, the same weariful and gloomy colouring, grays warming into brown, grays darkening towards black; and for sole sign of life, here and there, but at incredible intervals, a creek running in a canyon. The plains have a grandeur of their own; but here there is nothing but a contorted smallness. Except for the air, which was light and stimulating, there was not one good circumstance in that God-forsaken land.

ROBERT LOUIS STEVENSON
Across the Plains, 1879

MONUMENT ROCK, ECHO CANYON

. . . where sculptured gardens and impregnable rocky fortresses reveal "an epic written by Mother Nature in her most ecstatic humor—in her most majestic manifestations"

WEBER RIVER, ENTRANCE TO ECHO CANYON

TERRES MAUVAISES, UTAH

Beyond it the road enters the Echo Canyon itself. It is a narrow gorge between rocky walls that tower hundreds of feet above its uneven floor, along which the river runs with a stream as bright and clear as at its very source. Not simply a straight cut between its precipices of red-and-dark-stained stone, but a winding valley, with every turn presenting some new variation of its wonderful scenery. On the mountains that form its sides there is little verdure —only a dwarfed growth of pine scattered here and there, leaving the steeper portions of the rock bare and ragged in outline. Now and then there are little openings, where the great walls spread apart and little glades are formed; but these are no less picturesque than the wilder passages. There are memorable places here. Half-way down the gorge is Hanging Rock, where Brigham Young spoke to his deluded hundreds after their long pilgrimage, and pointed out to them that they approached their Canaan—preached the Mormons' first sermon in the "Promised Land." Full of all that is wild and strange, as is this rocky valley, seen even from the prosaic window of a whirling railway-car, what must it have been with the multitude of fanatics, stranger than all its strangeness, standing on its varied floor and looking up at the speaking prophet, whom they half believed, half feared? The weary multitude of half-excited, half-stolid faces turned toward the preacher; the coarse, strong, wild words of the leader echoing from the long-silent rocks—why has no one ever pictured for us all of the scene that could be pictured?

OLIVER B. BUNCE
Picturesque America, 1872

Fleeing religious persecution in Nauvoo, Illinois, thousands of Americans—members of the Church of the Latter-day Saints, known as Mormons—journeyed west to distant Deseret . . .

SALT LAKE

Salt Lake City wears a pleasant aspect to the emigrant or traveler, weary, dusty, and browned with a thousand miles of jolting, fording, camping, through the scorched and naked American desert. It is located mainly on the bench of hard gravel that slopes southward from the foot of the mountains toward the lake valley; the houses— generally small and of one story—are all built of adobe (sun-hardened brick), and have a neat and quiet look; while the uniform breadth of the streets (eight rods) and the "magnificent distances" usually preserved by the buildings (each block containing ten acres, divided into eight lots, giving a quarter of an acre for buildings and an acre for garden, fruit, etc., to each householder) make up an ensemble seldom equaled. Then the rills of bright, sparkling, leaping water which, diverted from the streams issuing from several adjacent mountain canyons, flow through each street and are conducted at will into every garden, diffuse an air of freshness and coolness which none can fail to enjoy, but which only a traveler in summer across the Plains can fully appreciate. On a single business street, the post office, principal stores, etc., are set pretty near each other, though not so close as in other cities; everywhere else, I believe, the original plan of the city has been wisely and happily preserved. Southward from the city, the soil is softer and richer, and there are farms of (I judge) ten to forty or sixty acres; but I am told that the lowest portion of the valley, nearly on a level with the lake, is so impregnated with salt, soda, etc., as to yield but a grudging return for the husbandman's labor. I believe, however, that even this region is available as a stock range—thousands on thousands of cattle, mainly owned in the city, being pastured here in winter as well as summer, and said to do well in all seasons.

HORACE GREELEY
An Overland Journey, 1859

NEW MORMON TEMPLE, SALT LAKE CITY

Who cares to go with the wagons?
Not we who are free and strong;
Our faith and arms, with right good will,
Shall pull our carts along.

A Mormon Song, 1856

. . . plodding on foot, pushing handcarts, guiding ox-drawn supply wagons, they finally attained the "Promised Land" in 1870. Their leader, Brigham Young declared, "This is the place!"

MORMONS CROSSING THE PLAINS

VIEWS ON MAIN STREET, SALT LAKE CITY

MORMON TABERNACLE

The American frontier never before beheld a movement quite like that of the Mormons. The authority of the Church was absolute. This discipline, when coupled with the wise leadership of Young, made the Mormon experiment a success. More than fifteen thousand people made their way to Utah from Nauvoo. The numbers in the mountain settlement steadily increased as converts poured in, coming particularly from England. The opportunity for material success and for independence on the American frontier was a powerful aid to the Mormon missionaries preaching to impoverished and despairing folk of the British Isles. Nor did the control of the Church end with the completion of the trek from Illinois. In Utah, Church and State were practically one and through the political as well as spiritual power of the Church controlled the economic and social life of the community. Natural leaders who arose among the people were rewarded by ecclesiastical office. Dissension was negligible. Only a community so disciplined and so forgetful of the individualistic characteristics of the American frontier could have established itself in the semi-arid edge of the Central Basin. The Mormon settlement is an illustration of the power of religion in moulding society.

Pageant of America, 1926

Picturesque buttes, carved cliffs, and monolithic canyons of vivid colors—created by emerging rivers of the Utah landscape plunging through shales and sandstones . . .

RED BUTTES, LARAMIE PLAINS

Only with the approach to Green River does the verdure come again—and then only here and there, generally close by the river-bank. Here the picturesque forms of the buttes reappear—a welcome relief to the monotony that has marked the outlook during the miles of level desert that are past. The distance, too, is changed, and no longer is like the great surface of a sea. To the north, forming the horizon, stretches the Wind-River Range—named with a breezy poetry that we miss in the later nomenclature of the race that has followed after the pioneers. To the south lie the Uintah Mountains.

The Church Butte is the grandest of the groups that rise in this singular and striking series of tower-like piles of stone. It lies somewhat further on, beyond the little station of Bryan, and forms a compact and imposing mass of rock, with an outlying spur that has even more than the main body the air of human, though gigantic architecture. It "imposes on the imagination," says Mr. Bowles, in one of his passages of clear description, "like a grand old cathedral going into decay—quaint in its crumbling ornaments, majestic in its height and breadth." And of the towering forms of the whole group, he says: "They seem, like the more numerous and fantastic illustrations of Nature's frolicksome art in Southern Colorado, to be the remains of granite hills that wind and water, and especially the sand whirlpools that march with lordly force through the air—literally moving mountains—have left to tell the story of their own achievements. Not unfitly, there as here, they have won the title of 'Monuments to the Gods.' "

E. L. BURLINGAME

Picturesque America, 1872

CHURCH BUTTE, UTAH

PLAINS OF THE HUMBOLDT

. . . evolved in "Monuments of the Gods"—the scenic wonderland where the plateau country is dotted with natural masterpieces in eerie formations

CLIFFS OF GREEN RIVER

The route of the Pacific Railway is not only that which for many years will be the most familiar path across the Plains, and not only that which passes nearest to the well-known emigrant-road of former days, but it is also the road which, though it misses the nobler beauties of the Rocky Mountains, shows the traveller the prairie itself in perhaps as true and characteristic an aspect as could be found on any less-tried course. It passes through almost every change of prairie scenery—the fertile land of the east and the alkali region farther on; past the historic outposts of the old pioneers; among low *buttes* and infrequent "islands;" and over a country abounding in points of view from which one may take in all the features that mark this portion of the continent. To the south, the great level expanse is hardly interrupted before the shore of the Gulf of Mexico is reached, and the Mexican boundary; to the north, the hills and high table-land of the Upper Missouri are the only breaks this side of the Canadian border. Through almost the middle of this vast and clear expanse the Union Pacific Railway runs east and west—a line of life flowing like a river through the great plain— the Kansas Pacific joining it at the middle of its course, a tributary of no small importance.

E. L. BURLINGAME

Picturesque America, 1872

DIAL ROCK, RED BUTTES, LARAMIE PLAINS

In the 1830s and 1840s, exploring expeditions were fortunate to have among them artists like Samuel Seymour, George Catlin, Carl Bodmer, and Alfred Jacob Miller

That grandeur was still to be found in the Far West; and as the explorer, the frontiersman, the hunter, the road builder, the homemaker pushed into the vast region beyond the Mississippi, many an American artist went along with his sketchbook to record the appearance and habits of the vanishing redskin. George Catlin journeyed from St. Louis up the Missouri River. His subjects ranged from prairie fires to a buffalo hunt on snowshoes, and his observation and daring broke through the limitations of his technique. Audiences here and in Europe marveled at Catlin's traveling exhibition, which included not only his many canvases but also a group of live Indians. Many others followed Catlin: John Mix Stanley painted from Texas to Oregon; Alfred J. Miller made fresh and brilliant water colors of the Rockies; Seth Eastman illustrated the six volumes of Henry Schoolcraft's work on the Indian tribes; a German-born artist named Albert Bierstadt joined the surveying expedition of General Lander and made the first of those great panoramic pictures of towering canyons, mighty waterfalls, redwood forests, and stupendous mountain peaks for which American millionaires were to pay fantastic prices. Thus was the natural setting of America presented in fresh, bold colors to its inhabitants.

OLIVER W. LARKIN
The Artist in the 19th Century, 1949

CHICAGO LAKE

PIKES PEAK, FROM GARDEN OF THE GODS

Later, the illustrated weeklies, and their staffs of graphic artists, did much to acquaint a nation hungry for information—with words and pictures of the fabulous West

MOUNTAIN OF THE HOLY CROSS

Not a great distance from here, leading down the mountain from Elk Lake, is a picturesque cascade, that finds its way through deep gorges and canyons to the Rio Grande. The Mountain of the Holy Cross is next reached. This is the most celebrated mountain in the region, but its height, which has been over-estimated, is not more than fourteen thousand feet. The ascent is exceedingly toilsome even for inured mountaineers, and I might give you an interesting chapter describing the difficulties that beset us. There is a very beautiful peculiarity in the mountain, as its name shows. The principal peak is composed of gneiss, and the cross fractures of the rock on the eastern slope have made two great fissures, which cut into one another at right angles, and hold their snow in the form of a cross the summer long.

W. H. RIDEING
Picturesque America, 1872

Main Street in the frontier towns: boxlike shanties and false fronts reflecting the slapdash haste of construction, a mix of saloons and hardware stores, bakeries and bordellos . . .

SITE OF SILVERTON R.R.   SILVER LAKE, COLORADO

BEAR CREEK FALLS

DONKEY PACK HAULING RAILS

. . .dominated by congested traffic churning helter-skelter: covered wagons and stagecoaches creating scenes of frenzied activity

MAIN STREET, LEADVILLE, COLORADO

MARKET SQUARE CONGESTION, PARIS, TEXAS

Going to town, by carriage or buggy, was a deeply ingrained American custom throughout the past century. In thousands of villages and towns, the highlight of the week was the family shopping trip on Saturday. Often the farmer, on such a visit, would trade his produce like eggs, fruit or vegetables for dry goods or household items needed at the general store . . .

. . . On Main Street U.S.A., the grain dealer's was a very important stop on the visiting farmer's busy schedule. His store was generally built around a wide driveway to allow hand-trucking of bags, barrels and bales. To one side of the entrance was usually a crudely improvised office, with a window for the display of grain samples. The simple placards told their story: "No. 1 Yellow corn"; "No. 2 White oats"; or "Fancy white middlings." His walls were often decorated with colorful lithos of famous race horses, agricultural calendars, black and white broadsides of a coming Fair, plus a sprinkling of patent feed posters. Over the owner's cluttered rolltop desk, there hung, more than likely, *The Horse Fair* . . . certainly a few *Currier and Ives* featuring the latest in horse-drawn carriages. The town livery stable was a scene of hectic activity. Here, while Farmer Jones did his trading, he also parked his horse and buggy, where for the sum of twenty-five cents his horse would be fed and watered. In the more progressive towns public tie-racks with feed troughs were provided, especially for those who arrived early.

CLARENCE P. HORNUNG

Wheels Across America, 1959

Many gold seekers—whose luck did not pan out—returned home or took to farming, irrigation projects helping to enrich the arid soil

RESULT OF IRRIGATION.

MAKING A START.

"Those whom we meet here coming down confirm the worst news we have had from the Peak. There is scarcely any gold there; those who dig cannot average two shillings per day; all who can get away are leaving; Denver and Auraria are nearly deserted; terrible sufferings have been endured on the Plains, and more must yet be encountered; hundreds would gladly work for their board, but cannot find employment—in short, Pike's Peak is an exploded bubble, which thousands must bitterly rue to the end of their days. Such is the tenor of our latest advices. I have received none this side of Leavenworth that contradict them. My informant says all are getting away who can, and that we shall find the region nearly deserted."

HORACE GREELEY

An Overland Journey, 1859

Soon the sun rose bright and clear; but the air was keen, with a stiff breeze eastward in our teeth. We were down in a wide depression of the Plains: but presently we rose up out of it, and as we struck the summit of the 'divide,' lo, the Rocky Mountains were before us in all their grandeur and sublimity. To the north rose Long's Peak, fourteen thousand feet above the sea, heaven-kissing, but with his nightcap still on; to the south, was Pike's Peak, eleven thousand feet above the sea, snow-crowned; while between, a hundred miles or more, swelled and towered the Mountains—at the base mere foot-hills, then ridge mounting on ridge and peak on peak, until over and above all the Snowy Range cropped out sublime.

JAMES F. RUSLING

Across America, 1874

LIFTING WHEELS
ON THE GUNNISON.

THE BAD LANDS.

IRRIGATION IN COLORADO

High up in the San Juan Mountains of southwestern Colorado —the nations's most mountainous state—gold, silver, lead, and other ores lured miners into almost impassable terrain

THE OLD UTE RESERVATION, COLORADO

Such was the actual state of things when the first flood of gold-seeking immigration began to pour in upon Auraria and Denver two months or more ago. Many of the seekers had left home with very crude ideas of gold-digging, impelled by glowing bulletins from writers who confounded sanguine expectations with actual results, and at best spoke of any casual realization of five to ten dollars from a day's washing as though it were a usual and reliable reward of gold-seeking industry throughout this region. Many who came were doubtless already wearied and disgusted with the hardships of their tedious journey—with sleeping in wet blankets through storms of snow and hurricanes of hail, and urging hollow and weary cattle over immense, treeless plains, on which the grass had hardly started. Coming in thus weather-beaten, chafed and soured, and finding but a handful of squalid adventurers living in the rudest log huts, barred out from the mountains by snow and ice, and precluded from washing the sands of the streams on the plains by high water, they jumped at once to the conclusion that the whole thing was a humbug, got up by reckless speculators to promote selfish ends.

HORACE GREELEY

An Overland Journey,

1859

Six to eight million years ago, when the Colorado River snaked its way across a sea-level plain, a giant upheaval of the land caused the waters to rush in . . .

Clouds are playing in the canyon to-day. Sometimes they roll down in great masses, filling the gorge with gloom; sometimes they hang aloft from wall to wall and cover the canyon with a roof of impending storm, and we can peer long distances up and down this canyon corridor, with its cloud-roof overhead, its walls of black granite, and its river bright with the sheen of broken waters. Then a gust of wind sweeps down a side gulch and, making a rift in the clouds, reveals the blue heavens, and a stream of sunlight pours in. Then the clouds drift away into the distance, and hang around crags and peaks and pinnacles and towers and walls, and cover them with a mantle that lifts from time to time and sets them all in sharp relief. Then baby clouds creep out of side canyons, glide around points, and creep back again into more distant gorges. Then clouds arrange in strata across the canyon, with intervening vista views to cliffs and rocks beyond. The clouds are children of the heavens, and when they play among the rocks they lift them to the region above.

JOHN WESLEY POWELL

Canyons of the Colorado, 1895

KANAB CANYON, NEAR THE JUNCTION

THE GRAND CANYON

The walls now are more than a mile in height—a vertical distance difficult to appreciate. Stand on the south steps of the Treasury building in Washington and look down Pennsylvania Avenue to the Capitol; measure this distance overhead, and imagine cliffs to extend to that altitude, and you will understand what is meant; or stand at Canal Street in New York and look up Broadway to Grace Church, and you have about the distance; or stand at Lake Street bridge in Chicago and look down to the Central Depot, and you have it again. A thousand feet of this is up through granite crags; then steep slopes and perpendicular cliffs rise one above another to the summit. The gorge is black and narrow below, red and gray and flaring above, with crags and angular projections on the walls, which, cut in many places by side canyons, seem to be a vast wilderness of rocks. Down in these grand, gloomy depths we glide, ever listening . . .

JOHN WESLEY POWELL

*. . . granular sand and silt chiseled deeply into Archean
rock strata of shale and limestone to form the Grand Canyon—
the most spectacular gorge in the New World—217 miles long*

THE INNER GORGE

Whenever the brink of the chasm is reached the chances
are that the sun is high and these abnormal effects in full
force. The canyon is asleep. Or it is under a spell of enchantment which gives its bewildering mazes an aspect still
more bewildering. Throughout the long summer forenoon
the charm which binds it grows in potency. At midday the
clouds begin to gather, first in fleecy flecks, then in cumuli,
and throw their shadows into the gulf. At once the scene
changes. The slumber of the chasm is disturbed. The
temples and cloisters seem to raise themselves half awake to
greet the passing shadow. Their wilted, drooping, flattened
faces expand into relief. The long promontories reach out
from the distant wall as if to catch a moment's refreshment
from the shade. The colors begin to glow; the haze loses its
opaque density and becomes more tenuous. The shadows
pass, and the chasm relapses into its dull sleep again. Thus
through the midday hours it lies in fitful slumber, overcome by the blinding glare and withering heat, yet respon-
sive to every fluctuation of light and shadow like a delicate
organism. As the sun moves far into the west the scene
again changes, slowly and imperceptibly at first, but afterwards more rapidly. In the hot summer afternoons the sky
is full of cloud-play and the deep flushes with ready
answers. The banks of snowy clouds pour a flood of light
sidewise into the shadows and light up the gloom of the
amphitheaters and alcoves, weakening the glow of the haze
and rendering visible the details of the wall faces. At
length, as the sun draws near the horizon, the great drama
of the day begins.

CLARENCE E. DUTTON

its own aloof, almost contemp-
ous, way it is nevertheless ex-
ordinarily beautiful—nature's
imate achievement in that
uthwestern Style which surpris-
gly executes great monolithic
rms, sometimes sculptural and
metimes architectural, in bright,
ultihued sandstone. About the
le there is nothing to suggest the
arm of the landscape which
lcomes man; instead, there is
ly the grandeur of something
werfully alien, indifferent, and
during, as though it had been
ade to please the eye and perhaps
en to soothe the spirit of some
eature older, as well as less tran-
ory, than . . .

JOSEPH WOOD KRUTCH
Grand Canyon, 1957

GRAND CANYON OF THE COLORADO, WITH AMPHITHEATRE AND SCULPTURED BUTTES

The unsurpassed beauty of the High Sierras, the enchantment of nature's monuments, were lost to overland travelers trudging through dangerous mountain passes of the Great Divide

In this region of hidden grandeur lies the ground of hope for those cosmopoltan tourists who complain that the world is a small place, full of hackneyed scenes, after all. So long as there is locked up here in our great mountain-chain such a glory as the few who have penetrated into its fortresses have described, even the mountaineer who fancies he has exhausted two continents, need never despair. One noble feature of the whole Sierra—of all of it save that which lies above the level of any vegetable life —is its magnificent forest-covering. It may well be doubted if the growth of forests of pine is ever seen in greater perfection than is found here. These tall, straight, noble shafts are the very king of trees. Covering the great slopes with a dense mantle of sombre green, they lend a wonderful dignity to the peaks, as one looks upon them from a distance; and, to one already in the forest, they seem the worthy guardians of the mountain-sides. They are magnificent in size, as they are admirable in proportion. No mast or spar ever shaped by men's hands exceeds the already perfect grace of their straight, unbroken trunks. They are things to study for their mere beauty as individual trees, apart from their effect upon the general landscape, which even without them would be wild and picturesque enough.

E. L. BURLINGAME

Picturesque America, 1872

DEVIL'S GATE, WEBER CANYON

Bound for California, in the winter of 1846-1847, the Donner Party— three family groups with sixteen children—suffered a gruesome tragedy: snowed-in, hunger-driven, the survivors resorted to cannibalism

DONNER LAKE, NEVADA

Nov. 20 [1846]

Came to this place [now called Donner Lake] on the 31st of last month. It snowed. We went on to the pass. The snow is so deep we were unable to find the road, when within 3 miles of the summit. Then turned back to this shanty on the Lake. . . . We now have killed most part of our cattle having to stay here untill next spring & live on poor beef without bread or salt. It snowed during the space of eight days with our little intermission, after our arrival here. . . .

[December] 25th

Snowed all night & snows yet rapidly. Great difficulty in geting wood. John & Edwd. has to get it. I am not able. Offered our prayers to God this Cherimass morning. The prospect is apalling but hope in God. *Amen.*

PATRICK BREEN

Diary of a member of the Donner Party

The loss of the Donner Party—within sight of their goal just west of the Nevada Territory—illustrated the terrors of travel through the High Sierras

Bring me men to match
my mountains,
Bring me men to match
my plains,
Men with empires in their
purpose,
And new eras in their
brains.

The plain man is the
basic clod
From which we grow the
demigod;
And in the average man
is curled
The hero stuff that rules
the world.

SAM WALTER FOSS

The Coming American,
1897

SAN JOAQUIN RIVER

LAKE TAHOE

Descending from the mountain passes, the fertile fields of the Golden State appear: orchards, citrus groves, vineyards, and farms—outpacing the nation in growth and vitality

SUMMIT OF THE SIERRAS

The machine has divorced man from the world of nature to which he belongs, and in the process he has lost in large measure the powers of contemplation with which he was endowed. A prerequisite for the preservation of the canons of humanism is a reestablishment of organic roots with our natural environment and, related to it, the evolution of ways of life which encourage contemplation and the search for truth and knowledge. The flower and vegetable garden, green grass, the fireplace, the primeval forest with its wondrous assemblage of living things, the uninhabited hilltop where one can silently look at the stars and wonder—all of these things and many others are necessary for the fulfillment of man's psychological and spiritual needs. To be sure, they are of no "practical value" and are seemingly unrelated to man's pressing need for food and living space. But they are as necessary to the preservation of humanism as food is necessary to the preservation of human life.

HARRISON BROWN

*In 1859, ten years after California's gold strike, the new
diggings at Gregory Gulch came in "with a whoop and a holler" as
thousands struck it rich in Colorado's golden era of mining*

And the Rocky Mountains, with their grand, aromatic forests, their grassy glades, their frequent springs, and dancing streams of the brightest, sweetest water, their pure, elastic atmosphere, and their unequalled game and fish, are destined to be a favorite resort and home of civilized man. I never visited a region where physical life could be more surely prolonged or fully enjoyed. Thousands who rush hither for gold will rush away again disappointed and disgusted, as thousands have already done; and yet the gold is in these mountains, and the right men will gradually unearth it. I shall be mistaken if two or three millions are not taken out this year, and some ten millions in 1860, though all the time there will be, as now, a stream of rash adventurers heading away from the diggings, declaring that there is no gold there, or next to none. So it was in California and in Australia; so it must be here, where the obstacles to be overcome are greater, and the facilities for getting home decidedly better. All men are not fitted by nature for gold-diggers; yet thousands will not realize this until they have been convinced of it by sore experience.

HORACE GREELEY

An Overland Journey, 1859

Making ready to leave the Winter camp.

Camp on the Mountains.

A Find.

Arrival of the first Stage.

MINING LIFE IN COLORADO

Golden California ...
Gateway on the Pacific

BRIDAL VEIL FALLS . . . EMIGRANTS'
LAST DAY ON THE PLAINS . . . GLACIER,
MTS. RITTER AND LYELL . . . SAN
LORENZO CREEK . . . TOLTEC GORGE . . .
TUOLUMNE RIVER . . . MT. SHASTA . . .
"WILDCAT CASCADES" . . . SUTTER'S MILL
. . . COLOMA . . . AMERICAN RIVER . . .
CALIFORNIA GOLD DIGGERS . . . SAN
FRANCISCO . . . CENTRAL PACIFIC R. R.
TERMINUS . . .MARKET STREET . . . SANSOME
STREET . . . NEW CITY HALL . . . MARIN
COUNTY COAST . . . MENDOCINO . . . SEAL
ROCKS . . . MOUNT TAMALPAIS . . . MONTEREY
. . . HOTEL DEL MONTE . . . CYPRESS DRIVE
. . . CARMEL MISSION . . . SEQUOIA TREES . . .
MARIPOSA GROVE . . . YOSEMITE FALL . . .
CATHEDRAL SPIRES . . . GORGE OF THE
MERCED . . . HALF DOME . . . SENTINEL ROCK
AND FALLS . . . LOS ANGELES . . . STREETS AND
RESIDENCES . . . SANTA BARBARA MISSIONS

BRIDAL VEIL FALLS

Golden California...
Gateway on the Pacific

DURING THE GREAT AGE OF EXPLORA-
tion in the sixteenth century,
Europeans were beguiled with tales
of exotic and fabulously rich lands
on the other side of the globe. One such land
was an island of rocks and gold ruled by an
Amazon queen, Califía. Her realm was
described in a popular novel of the 1530s, and
despite its clearly fictional existence, the island
did resemble lands real, imagined, and a little
of both, which were rumored to have been
sighted across the seas. In 1535, Hernán Cortés
landed on a rugged peninsula off the Mexican
coast which reminded him of Queen Califía's
island. He named the land "California"; and
so, long before it would actually be explored

or settled, this rich and beautiful land had
found its name in the sort of legend that for
three centuries would draw people to her.

California has always inspired the wildest
dreams, and its reality has always exceeded
those dreams. The land was richer and far
more awesome than Califía's fabled island,
and the miners' gold would seem trifling compared to the fortunes that were made after the
gold gave out.

California has been described as a "sudden
land," where the mountains meet the sea and
do not slope down gently to it as they do on
the East Coast. Below Monterey the Santa
Lucia Mountains rise some eight hundred feet
above the water at Big Sur, and at sunset these

cliffs become a sheer plate of golden rock.

It is also a land of superlatives. Just east of Los Angeles is the highest peak in the continental United States, Mount Whitney, and the lowest point, Death Valley. South of the Oregon border stand some of the oldest and tallest trees on earth, the redwoods; while to the east lies the desolate lava country of the Modoc Plateau. Between the lofty Sierra Nevada and Coastal ranges lies the great Central Valley—four hundred fifty miles of flat farm land.

The Spanish came first to California in the 1540s, but did not find the gold they sought. More than two and a half centuries would pass before they would return in earnest. In 1770, Gaspar de Portolá established a garrison at Monterey, the city that would eventually become the Spanish capital of California. Just a year before, a lame and aging friar, Junípero Serra, had set off on muleback up the Baja peninsula to establish missions. Within a few years he had established twenty-one of them, all along the coast.

In 1821, after a protracted struggle, Spain granted Mexico its independence. The new republic included California, and since it was virtually uninhabited, the Mexican government awarded large tracts of land there to retired soldiers. The romantic era of the "ranchos" was extravagant, but short-lived. In 1846-1847 the war between Mexico and the United States, fought chiefly over possession of Texas, resulted in American acquisition of California. Still there were few inhabitants in the American settlements.

In 1848 James Marshall, working at Sutter's Mill, a small settlement in the north, discovered gold in the American River. Gold fever swept the East. Within four years the population of California increased sixfold, and regular steamship service between Boston and New York and San Francisco had begun, using the Isthmus of Panama as a transshipment point for passengers. San Francisco, up until then a small village called Yerba Buena, became something close to a metropolis. In 1849 alone, some five hundred fifty vessels arrived at her port, carrying some forty thousand passengers. The overland route, despite its hardships, became so popular that guidebooks were published for travelers along its two-thousand-mile route. By 1850 California had become a state, America's thirty-first.

The gold-digging in California lasted only some five years, but discoveries in the Northwest and in Nevada throughout the 1850s continued to draw prospectors and others to the port of San Francisco. In these years San Francisco was a lawless and raucous town. But as the population grew and settled, and as fortunes accumulated, it developed worldly amenities to accompany the more boisterous attractions of its Barbary Coast dancehalls and saloons. Comfortable, cosmopolitan, and cultured, San Francisco became America's Western capital. Frequently hidden in fog, but sometimes bathed in a light of Mediterranean clarity, its wind-shaped pines and gingerbread Gothic houses follow the angle of hills that dip gracefully toward the bay and the sea. San Francisco burned to the ground twice in the 1850s and again after an earthquake in 1906. But it always recovered, rebuilt more splendidly, and attracted a steady migration from Europe, the Orient, and the American East. Shaped by the wide-open, flamboyant spirit of its Gold Rush heritage, San Francisco calls itself "the city that knows how." By common assent, it does.

Dreams of gold first drew people to San Francisco. Dreams of agricultural riches drew people south, to Los Angeles. Its growth was slower than San Francisco's, but wild speculation in land—much of which was only desert—increased Los Angeles's population from the fifteen hundred counted in the census of 1850 to over eleven thousand by 1880. By the end of the 1880s, however, speculation faltered and thousands of disappointed migrants turned back east, or traveled north. Still, growth continued, if at a slower rate. Some came to farm, but many more came to enjoy a climate reputed to cure almost any ill. Los Angeles, San Diego, Santa Barbara, San Bernardino were already established towns by the turn of the nineteenth century, and they shared the influx of health-seekers with newer spas like Palm Springs, Pasadena, and Santa Monica.

Within half a century after its founding the United States stretched from the Atlantic to the Pacific. The destiny sought in the West was achieved by hardship, cruelty, and a perseverance that has always defied complete comprehension. But standing on Yosemite's snowy peaks, or looking out over a glistening San Francisco Bay, it is possible to glimpse the vision that lured a people west.

*California . . .El Dorado . . .land of golden promise—
hope and heartbreak of many, from the argonauts of '49
to the many millions who followed, by land and sea . . .*

They came by wagon and by horseback. Some 16,000 sailed around the Horn, a six months' voyage considerably longer than halfway around the world. Others—the more energetic —sailed to Chagres, threaded the Panamanian jungles by foot or muleback, and completed the six weeks' journey by ship. They arrived singly and in companies, with or without guidebooks, these young men from China, Peru, Mexico, and Europe; from the neat little towns of New England and the farm lands of Ohio. Most of those who came by ship were city men, described by Bancroft as "editors, ministers, traders, the briefless lawyer, starving student, the quack, the idler, the harlot, the gambler, the henpecked husband, the disgraced . . ." Among them were also many honest men and devoted women. Those who made the 2000 mile journey westward from the marshaling points in Missouri were largely farmers and mechanics— experienced frontiersmen. By the end of 1849 the population of California had skyrocketed to 100,000 exclusive of native Indians. Of this number the vast majority were somewhere between Sutter's Fort and the various mines at such places as Red Dog, Poker Flat, Rough and Ready, or Hell's Delight. They were in possession of what remained of the $10,000,000 pried from the earth that year. With the arrival of the bulk of those who had left home in '49, the value of the pannings jumped to $41,000,000—to double that amount in 1851.

SCOTT O'DELL

*The Romance of North
America, 1958*

CALIFORNIA EMIGRANTS' LAST DAY ON THE PLAINS

. . . making their arduous way across the continent, the Isthmus of Panama, or around the Horn—lured by the magnetic pull of land gracious in climate, rich in resources

Even on a map the state looks odd. Four of the boundary lines are as straight as a surveyor's eye can make them. The fifth is the huge wriggling gorge that the Colorado has cut for itself. The sixth boundary is stupefying. It is the Pacific Ocean. The California Current and millions of years of savage storm waves and winds have worked at the western edge of California. This line is made up of jagged inlets, irregular sandbars, unlikely harbors, long white beaches. It changes constantly; every year some of the tall soft cliffs tumble into the ocean and part of California is gone. Most rates are fairly uniform in climate and terrain, and this tends to make their citizens somewhat similar. California has few uniformities— and fantastic differences. Part is white, hot desert, part perpetual snow, part subtropical and part heavily wooded with pine and oak and redwood. It has an active volcano. It has a place called Bagdad where a man looked into the sky for 767 days for rain and was rewarded by a touch of wet on the 768th day. This was the longest unofficially recorded dry period in America. But another man, at Hoegees Camp, stood unbelievingly as it rained twenty-six inches in a single day and watched the deluge melt mountains into soft mud. Huge redwoods slid down slick canyons, and enormous boulders came loose with a large suck and ponderously, surrounded by tons of mud, crashed down on the redwoods.

EUGENE BURDICK

"Gold from the American River" was President Polk's message to Congress, December 5, 1848—electrifying news that changed the life of a nation, as eager adventurers came from all points of the compass

One morning in January [1848]—it was a clear cold morning; I shall never forget that morning—as I was taking my usual walk along the race, after shutting off the water my eye was caught by a glimpse of something shining in the bottom of the ditch. There was about a foot of water running there. I reached my hand down and picked it up; it made my heart thump, for I felt certain it was gold. The piece was about half the size of the shape of a pea. Then I saw another piece in the water. After taking it out I sat down and began to think right hard. I thought it was gold, and yet it did not seem to be of the right color; all the gold coin I had seen was of a reddish tinge; this looked more like brass. I recalled to mind all the metals I had ever seen or heard of, but I could find none that resembled this. Suddenly the idea flashed across my mind that it might be iron pyrites. I trembled to think of it! This question could soon be determined. Putting one of the pieces on hard river stone, I took another and commenced hammering it. It was soft and didn't break; it therefore must be gold, but largely mixed with some other metal, very likely silver; for pure gold, I thought, would certainly have a brighter color . . . .

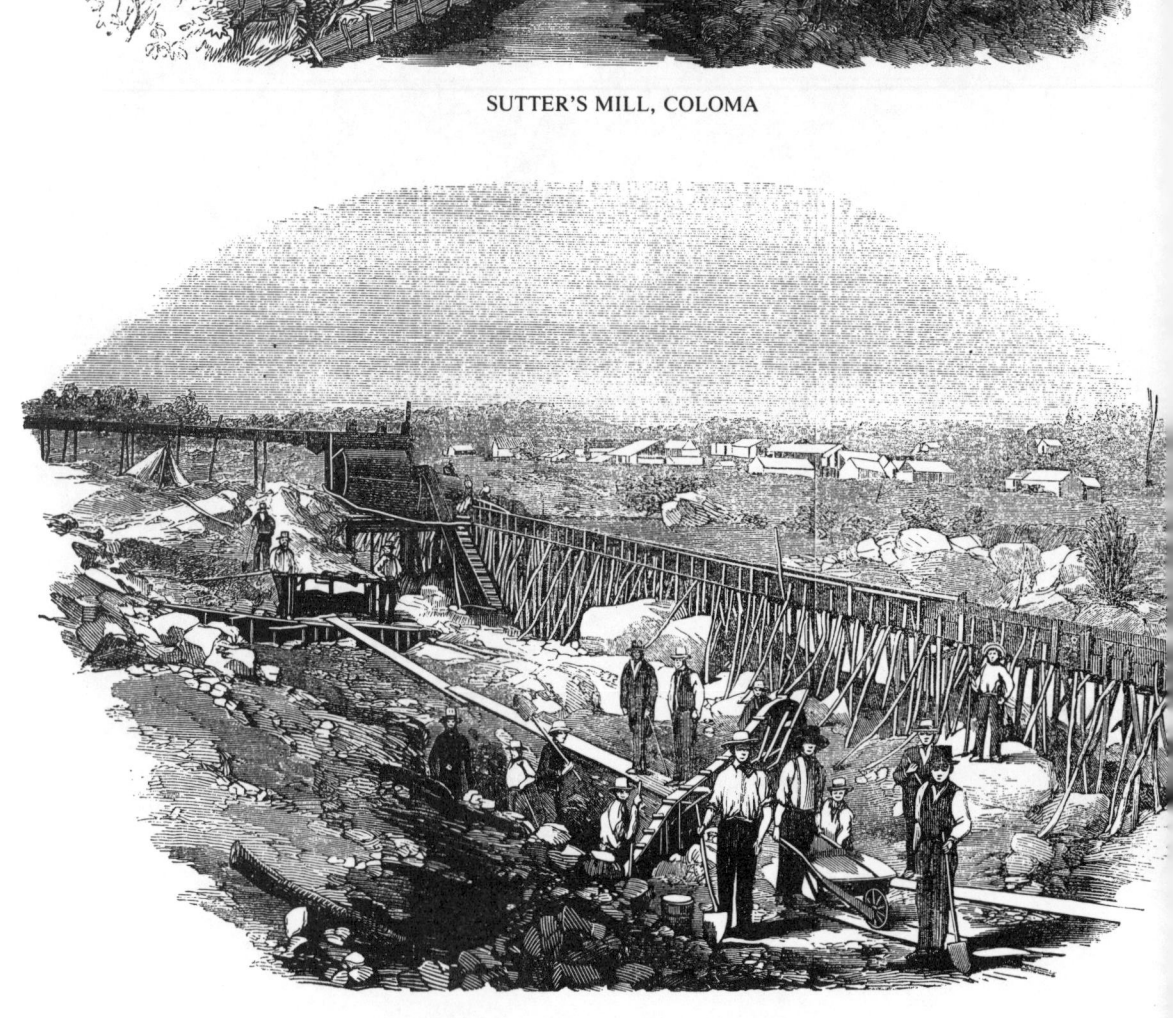

SUTTER'S MILL, COLOMA

PARKS' BAR COMPANY WORKS AND FLUME

Gold fever swept the nation. Wrote Walter Alton: "The blacksmith dropped his hammer, the carpenter his plane, the mason his trowel, the farmer his sickle, the baker his loaf. All were off for the mines"

NORTH FORK, AMERICAN RIVER

. . . When I returned to our cabin for breakfast I showed the two pieces to my men. They were all a good deal excited, and had they not thought that the gold only existed in small quantities they would have abandoned everything and left me to finish the job alone. However, to satisfy them, I told them that as soon as we had the mill finished we would devote a week or two to gold hunting and see what we could make out of it. While we were working in the race after this discovery, we always kept a sharp lookout, and in the course of three or four days we had picked up about three ounces—our work still progressing as lively as ever. JAMES MARSHALL

Account of the Discovery of Gold, 1848

CALIFORNIA GOLD DIGGERS

San Francisco—frontier fort, presidio, and mission, surrounded by a village of friendly Indians—visited by Richard Dana in 1835— gave promise of becoming "a place of great importance"

The city of San Francisco is built along the eastern base and up the side of a row of high sand hills, which stretch southwardly from the Golden Gate, between the Pacific Ocean on the west and the bay of San Francisco on the east. The city has been built out into the bay some fifty to a hundred rods by carting in sand from the eastern slope of the hills, which are thus left more abrupt than they originally were. The compactly built district seems rather more than two miles north and south, by somewhat less east and west. I judge that the city is destined to expand in the main southwardly, or along the bay, avoiding the steep ascent toward the west. The county covers 26,000 acres, of which one-half will probably be covered in time by buildings or country seats. I estimate the present population at about 80,000. It seems not to have increased very rapidly for some years past, and this is as it should be. San Francisco has the largest trade of any city on the Pacific; but as yet she is the emporium of California and Oregon only. A railroad communication with the Atlantic states would make her the New York of this mighty ocean—the focus of the trade of all America west of the Andes and Rocky Mountains, and of Polynesia as well, with an active and increasing Australian commerce . . .

WESTERN TERMINUS, CENTRAL PACIFIC RAILROAD, SAN FRANCISCO

MARKET STREET, SAN FRANCISCO

*Dana's vision materialized with news of gold's discovery—
an instant metropolis mushroomed, devastated many times by fire,
rebuilt each time as soon as flames died and embers cooled*

NEW CITY HALL, SAN FRANCISCO

. . . Without an inter-oceanic railroad, she must grow slowly, because the elements of her trade have been measured and their limits nearly reached. The gold product of this region has for years averaged about fifty millions per annum, and is not likely soon to rise much above that amount. That sum does not require, and will not create, a larger mart than San Francisco now is.

HORACE GREELEY
An Overland Journey, 1859

San Francisco has some fine buildings, but is not a well-built city—as, indeed, how could she be? She is hardly yet ten years old, has been three or four times in good part laid in ashes, and is the work mainly of men of moderate means, who have paid higher for the labor they required than she ever paid elsewhere for putting so much wood, stone, brick and mortar into habitations or stores. Her growth for the first five years of her existence was very rapid; but Pottsville, Chicago, Liverpool have also had rapid growths, and St. Louis is now expanding faster than this city has done since 1852. Cities are created and enlarged by the wants of populations outside of their own limits; San Francisco will take another start when she shall have become beneficent if not indispensable to a much larger radius than that now buying and selling mainly through her. In the hope that the time for this is not far distant, I bid her God speed.

HORACE GREELEY
An Overland Journey, 1859

SANSOME STREET, SAN FRANCISCO

John Charles Fremont, flamboyant freebooter and explorer, precipitated the seizure of Spanish California, acquiring, without bloodshed, the regions then loosely held by Mexico

The Bay of San Francisco is separated by the sea by low mountain ranges. Looking from the peaks of the Sierra Nevada, the coast mountains present an apparently continuous line, with only a single gap, resembling a mountain pass. This is the entrance to the great bay, and is the only water communication from the coast to the interior country. Approaching from the sea, the coast presents a bold outline. On the south, the bordering mountains come down in a narrow ridge of broken hills, terminating in a precipitous point, against which the sea breaks heavily. On the northern side, the mountain presents a bold promontory, rising in a few miles to a height of two or three thousand feet. Between these points is the strait—about one mile broad in the narrowest part, and five miles long from the sea to the bay. To this Gate I gave the name of *Chrysopylar,* or GOLDEN GATE; for the same reasons that the harbor of Byzantium (Constantinople afterwards), was called *Chrysoceras,* or GOLDEN HORN. Passing through this gate, the bay opens to the right and left, extending in each direction about thirty-five miles, having a total length of more than seventy, and a coast of about two hundred and seventy-five miles . . .

PACIFIC COAST SCENE, MARIN COUNTY

COAST OF MENDOCINO

*He described the Golden Gate and California coastline:
"a varied character of rugged and broken hills, rolling land,
and rich alluvial shores backed by fertile and wooded ranges"*

SEAL ROCKS, SAN FRANCISCO

. . . It is divided, by straits and projecting points, into three separate bays, of which the northern two are called San Pablo and Suisoon Bays. Within, the view presented is of a mountainous country, the bay resembling an interior lake of deep water, lying between parallel ranges of mountains. Islands, which have the bold character of the shores—some mere masses of rock, and others grass-covered, rising to the height of three and eight hundred feet—break its surface, and add to its picturesque appearance.

JOHN CHARLES FREMONT
A Year of American Travel,
1878

MOUNT TAMALPAIS AND RED PORCH

Every day of my life at Big Sur I had before me the incomparable vista of the Pacific. Its everchanging aspects offered me alternately peace and stimulation. I had to learn to live with this overwhelming force which is hidden within its obvious grandeur.

HENRY MILLER
My Life and Times, 1971

Monterey—secure fort, presidio, and provincial capital of the California area since its founding in 1770—grew in importance after Mexican Independence, in 1821, luring settlers and traders . . .

In Monterey there are a number of English and Americans (English or "Ingles" all are called who speak the English language) who have married Californians, become united to the Catholic Church, and acquired considerable property. Having more industry, frugality, and enterprise than the natives, they soon get nearly all the trade into their hands. They usually keep shops, in which they retail the goods purchased in larger quantities from our vessels, and also send a good deal into the interior, taking hides in pay, which they again barter with our vessels. In every town on the coast there are foreigners engaged in this kind of trade, while I recollect but two shops kept by natives. The people are naturally suspicious of foreigners, and they would not be allowed to remain were it not they they become good Catholics, and by marrying natives and bringing up their children as Catholics and Spaniards and not teaching them the English language, they quiet suspicion and even become popular and leading men. The chief alcaldes in Monterey and Santa Barbara were both Yankees by birth.

RICHARD HENRY DANA, JR.
Two Years before the Mast,
1840

THE OLD CUSTOM HOUSE.

CLIFF NEAR CYPRESS DRIVE.

CHINESE FISHING BOAT.

THE "ARGUS" OFFICE.

MONTEREY, CARMEL AND VICINITY

. . . who sailed up and down the Pacific coast, visiting settlements,
—offering a wide assortment of household goods and knickknacks
to Californios, *hungry for more of life's amenities*

ARIZONA GARDEN — CACTI 13 FT HIGH.

HOTEL DELMONTE.

CHINESE FISHING VILLAGE.

CARMEL MISSION—EST. 1770.

Four generations have seen few changes in the Spanish quarter of the town; yet, in the last decade, Monterey has become one of the great popular resorts of the Pacific coast, and every year sees thousands of tourists enjoy its varied scenery and its equable climate. It boasts of one of the finest hotels in the country; it prides itself on the magnificent seventeen-mile drive which has been laid out through the dark pine woods and along the shore of the Pacific. After the scenery—which seems to possess a perennial charm, giving the visitor fresh surprises every morning—there is nothing more attractive about Monterey than this dreamy Spanish life that takes no count of time or progress, the changes of governments or the new discoveries of science. Sleepy as the old town looks in its mid-day siesta, it has had a stirring history. It was founded by Junipero Serra, the leader of the Franciscan monks who established the chain of missions along the California coast, and for fifty years created there the idyllic pastoral life, now seen only in the poet's dream of Arcadia. The Bay of Monterey witnessed the arrival of stout Spanish troopers from Mexico, the building of a rude fort on the hill that overlooks the town, and the establishment of the seat of government of Alta California.

J. R. FITCH

Picturesque California, 1888

"Great trees and groves," declared John Muir, one of
America's revered naturalists, *"need to be venerated
as sacred monuments and halls of council and worship . . .*

The Big Tree (*Sequoia gigantea*) is nature's forest masterpiece, and, as far as I know, the greatest of living things. It belongs to an ancient stock, as its remains in old rocks show, and has a strange air of other days about it, a thoroughbred look inherited from the long ago, the auld land syne of trees. Once the genus was common, and with many species flourished in the now desolate Arctic regions, the interior of North America, and in Europe; but in long eventful wanderings from climate to climate only two species have survived the hardships they had to encounter, the *gigantea* and *sempervirens:* the former now restricted to the western slopes of the Sierra, the other to the Coast Mountains, and both to California, excepting a few groves of redwood which extend into Oregon. The Pacific coast in general is the paradise of conifers. Here nearly all of them are giants, and display a beauty and magnificence unknown elsewhere. The climate is mild, the ground never freezes, and moisture and sunshine abound all the year. Nevertheless, it is not easy to account for the colossal size of the Sequoias. The largest are about three hundred feet high, and thirty feet in diameter.

JOHN MUIR

*My First Summer in the
Sierra, 1911*

THE SEQUOIAS—GIANT TREES OF CALIFORNIA

*"but soon after the discovery of the Calaveras Grove,
one of the grandest trees was cut down by laborious vandals
for the sake of the stump—to be used as a dance floor!"*

o description can give any adequate idea of
eir singular majesty, much less of their beauty.
cepting the sugar pine, most of its neighbors
th pointed tops seem to be forever shouting
Excelsior!" while the Big Tree, though soaring
ove them all, seems satisfied, its rounded head
·ised lightly as a cloud, giving no impression
 trying to go higher. Only in youth does it
ow, like other conifers, a heavenward yearning
enly aspiring with a long quick-growing top.
deed, the whole tree, for the first century or
o, or until a hundred to a hundred and fifty
et high, is arrowhead in form, and, compared
th the solemn rigidity of age, is as sensitive to
e wind as a squirrel tail. The lower branches
e gradually dropped, as it grows older, and the
pper ones thinned out, until comparatively few
e left. These, however, are developed to great
ze, divide again and again, and terminate in
ossy rounded masses of leafy branchlets, while
e head becomes dome-shaped. Then, poised in
illness of strength and beauty, stern and
olemn in mien, it glows with eager, enthusiastic
·e, quivering to the tip of every leaf and
·anch and far-reaching root, calm as a granite
ome,—the first to feel the touch of the rosy
·ams of the morning, the last to bid the sun
ood-night.

JOHN MUIR

My First Summer in the Sierra, 1911

BIG TREES, MARIPOSA GROVE

FALLEN SEQUOIA

It is a curious fact that all the very old Sequoias
have lost their heads by lightning. "All things
come to him who waits;" but of all living things
Sequoia is perhaps the only one able to wait
long enough to make sure of being struck by
lightning. Thousands of years it stands ready
and waiting, offering its head to every passing
cloud as if inviting its fate, praying for heaven's
fire as a blessing; and when at last the old head
is off, another of the same shape immediately
begins to grow on. Every bud and branch seems
excited, like bees that have lost their queen, and
tries hard to repair the damage. Branches that
for many centuries have been growing out hori-
zontally at once turn upward, and all their
branchlets arrange themselves with reference to a
new top of the same peculiar curve as the old
one.

JOHN MUIR

70

Yosemite—land of enchantment, and a botanist's paradise—with peaks and precipices of infinite immensity, Yosemite Falls, with a drop of almost fifteen hundred feet, a height nine times that of Niagara . . .

We set out from Yosemite about the end of August, and our first camp was made in the well-known Mariposa Grove. Here and in the adjacent pine woods I spent nearly a week, carefully examining the boundaries of the grove for traces of its greater extension without finding any. Then I struck out into the majestic trackless forest to the southeastward, hoping to find new groves or traces of old ones in the dense silver fir and pine woods about the head of Big Creek, where soil and climate seemed most favorable to their growth; but not a single tree or old monument of any sort came to light until I climbed the high rock called Wamellow by the Indians. Here I obtained telling views of the fertile forest-filled basin of the upper Fresno. Innumerable spires of the noble yellow pine were displayed rising one above another on the braided slopes, and yet nobler sugar pines with superb arms outstretched in the rich autumn light, while away toward the southwest, on the verge of the glowing horizon, I discovered the majestic dome-like crowns of Big Trees towering high over all, singly and in close grove congregations.

JOHN MUIR
The Yosemite, 1912

CATHEDRAL SPIRES

. . . owes its establishment as one of the nation's most popular parks largely to the voice and efforts of John Muir— naturalist, explorer, and environmentalist extraordinaire

YOSEMITE FALLS

Then your eye is smitten by the marvel of Yosemite Falls. You stand entranced while a river rushes out of the blue in great spurts like the throbbing of the heart of the earth. You see it fall half a mile in a rock-shaking torrent into a land of soft beauty that differs from the snowy regions of the Valley's rim as Italy differs from Norway. One never wearies of watching the comets or rockets of water whitened by the friction of the air. They are continually forming, shooting downward and either exploding or fading into mist-wraiths before the end of the first clear plunge of twenty-six hundred feet. These rockets descend much faster than the main masses; and when the air is filled with them, one might almost imagine oneself witnessing the collapse of some roof-ful of gypsum flowers and alabaster stalactites in one of the "cities" of Mammoth Cave. On certain heavy days this fall is peculiarly effective, as when a broad white wreath of cloud festoons itself along the top of the crag, and the torrent, alike in hue, gushes out of it like a vast beard gushing down from a huge mustache. Or, to vary the figure, one might fancy that some cyclopean distillery were busy condensing that cloud and pouring the product immediately into the vat of the Valley. It is as though nature were giving so simple a laboratory demonstration of her methods that every child might grasp the workings of her divine chemistry.

ROBERT HAVEN SCHAUFFLER
Romantic America, 1913

The battle, in 1854, to protect Yosemite's renowned scenic wonders from the cattleman's invasion and public abuse—later led by John Muir —halted the encroachment of lumber and logging interests, and . . .

I cannot stop to give my impressions of Yosemite here, further than to say that, as contrasted with the Grand Canyon, one could live in Yosemite and find life sweet. It is like a great house in which one could find a nook where he could make his nest, looked down upon by the gods of the granite ages. The floor of the Valley really has a domestic, habitable look, with its orchards and ploughed lands, its superb trees, and its limpid, silently gliding river; and above all, its waterfalls fluttering against the granite precipices. The ethereal beauty of waterfalls, and the genial look of the pure streams, make almost any place habitable.

JOHN BURROUGH

The Writings of John Burroughs, 1904-1

GORGE OF THE MERCED,
FROM GLACIER POINT TRAIL

HALF DOME

I shall not multiply details, nor waste paper in noting all the foolish names which foolish people have given to different peaks or turrets. Just think of two giant stone towers, or pillars, which rise a thousand feet above the towering cliff which form their base, being styled the Two Sisters! Could anything be more maladroit and lackadaisical? The Dome is a high, round, naked peak, which rises between the Merced and its little tributary from the inmost recesses of the Sierra Nevada already instanced, and which towers to an altitude of over five thousand feet above the waters at its base. Picture to yourself a perpendicular wall of bare granite nearly or quite one mile high! Yet there are some dozen or score of peaks in all, ranging from three thousand to five thousand feet above the valley, and a biscuit tossed from any of them would strike very near its base, and its fragments go bounding and falling still further. I certainly miss here the glaciers of Chamonix, but I know no single wonder of nature on earth which can claim a superiority over the Yosemite. Just dream yourself for one hour in a chasm nearly ten miles long, with egress, save for birds and water, but at three points, up the face of precipices from three thousand to four thousand feet high, the chasm scarcely more than a mile wide at any point, and tapering to a mere gorge, or canyon, at either end, with walls of mainly naked and perpendicular white granite, from three thousand to five thousand feet high, so that looking up to the sky from it is like looking out of an unfathomable profound—and you will have some conception of the Yosemite.

HORACE GREELEY

An Overland Journey, 1859

. . . became a landmark victory of the conservationists, establishing a national park of infinite natural resources, as a legacy for the enjoyment of future generations

d here let me renew my tribute to the
velous bounty and beauty of the forests of
whole mountain region. The Sierra Nevadas
the glorious glaciers, the frequent rains, the
verdure, the abundant cataracts of the Alps;
they far surpass them—they surpass any
r mountains I ever saw—in the wealth and
e of their trees. Look down from almost any
heir peaks, and your range of vision is filled,
nded, satisfied, by what might be termed a
pest-tossed sea of evergreens, filling every
nd valley, covering every hillside, crowning
y peak but the highest, with their unfading
riance. That I saw during this day's travel
y hundreds of pines eight feet in diameter,
cedars at least six feet, I am confident; and
e were miles after miles of such a smaller
s of like genus standing as thick as they
d grow. Steep mountainsides, allowing them
row, rank above rank, without obstructing
other's sunshine, seem peculiarly favorable
he production of these serviceable giants. But
Summit Meadows are peculiar in their heavy
ge of balsam fir of all sizes, from those bare-
ne foot high to those hardly less than two
dred, their branches surrounding them in
ars, their extremities gracefully bent down by
weight of winter snows, making them here, I
confident, the most beautiful trees on earth.
dry promontories which separate these
dows are also covered with a species of
ce, which is only less graceful than the fir
esaid. I never before enjoyed such a tree-
t as on this wearing, difficult ride.

SENTINEL ROCK AND FALLS

FOOT OF SENTINEL FALLS

It is not the Merced River that makes this fall, but a mere tributary trout brook, which pitches in from the north by a barely once-broken descent of two thousand six hundred feet, while the Merced enters the valley at its eastern extremity, over falls of six hundred and two hundred and fifty feet. But a river thrice as large as the Merced, at this season, would be utterly dwarfed by all the other accessories of this prodigious chasm. Only a Mississippi or a Niagara could be adequate to their exactions. I readily concede that a hundred times the present amount of water may roll down the Yosemite Fall in the months of May and June, when the snows are melting from the central ranges of the Sierra Nevada, which bound this abyss on the east; but this would not add a fraction to the wonder of this vivid exemplification of the divine power and majesty. At present, the little stream that leaps down the Yosemite, and is all but shattered to mist by the amazing descent, looks like a tapeline let down from the cloud-capped height to measure the depth of the abyss. The Yosemite Valley (or Gorge) is the most unique and majestic of nature's marvels, but the Yosemite Fall is of little account. Were it absent, the valley would not be perceptibly less worthy of a fatiguing visit.

HORACE GREELEY

An Overland Journey, 1859

The Sierra Nevada—backbone and chain of mountains endowing California with picturesque and dramatic natural spectacles, endless in variety and richness . . .

Once in a lifetime, if one is lucky, one so merges with sunlight and air and running water that whole eons, the eons that mountains and deserts know, might pass in a single afternoon without discomfort. The mind has sunk away into its beginnings among old roots and the obscure tricklings and movings that stir inanimate things . . . . one can never quite define this secret; but it has something to do, I am sure, with common water. Its substance reaches everywhere; it touches the past and prepares the future; it moves under the poles and wanders thinly in the heights of air. It can assume forms of exquisite perfection in a snowflake, or strip the living to a single shining bone cast up by the sea.

LOREN EISELEY

MOUNT LYELL GROUP, FROM TUOLUMNE RIVER

The home ranch from which we set out is on the south side of the Tuolumne River near French Bar, where the foothills of metamorphic gold-bearing slates dip below the stratified deposits of the Central Valley. We had not gone more than a mile before some of the old leaders of the flock showed by the eager, inquiring way they ran and looked ahead that they were thinking of the high pastures they had enjoyed last summer. Soon the whole flock seemed to be hopefully excited, the mothers calling their lambs, the lambs replying in tones wonderfully human, their fondly quavering calls interrupted now and then by hastily snatched mouthfuls of withered grass. Amid all this seeming babel of baas as they streamed over the hills every mother and child recognized each other's voice. In case a tired lamb, half asleep in the smothering dust, should fail to answer, its mother would come running back through the flock toward the spot whence its last response was heard, and refused to be comforted until she found it, the one of a thousand, though to our eyes and ears all seemed alike.

JOHN MUIR

MOUNT SHASTA

. . . a gentle wilderness, made accessible through decades
of persistent efforts of dedicated conservationists, led by the energy
of John Muir and the Sierra Club he founded, in 1892

In the great Central Valley of California there are only two seasons—spring and summer. The spring begins with the first rainstorm, which usually falls in November. In a few months the wonderful flowery vegetation is in full bloom, and by the end of May it is dead and dry and crisp, as if every plant had been roasted in an oven. Then the lolling, panting flocks and herds are driven to the high, cool, green pastures of the Sierra. I was longing for the mountains about this time, but money was scarce and I couldn't see how a bread supply was to be kept up. While I was anxiously brooding on the bread problem, so troublesome to wanderers, and trying to believe that I might learn to live like the wild animals, gleaning nourishment here and there from seeds, berries, etc., sauntering and climbing in joyful independence of money or baggage, Mr. Delaney, a sheepowner, for whom I had worked a few weeks, called on me, and offered to engage me to go with his shepherd and flock to the headwaters of the Merced and Tuolumne Rivers—the very region I had most in mind. I was in the mood to accept work of any kind that would take me into the mountains whose treasures I had tasted last summer in the Yosemite region. The flock, he explained, would be moved gradually higher through the successive forest belts as the snow melted, stopping for a few weeks at the best places we came to. These I thought would be good centers of observation from which I might be able to make many telling excursions within a radius of eight or ten miles of the camps to learn something of the plants, animals, and rocks; for he assured me that I should be left perfectly free to follow my studies. I judged, however, that I was in no way the right man for the place, and freely explained my shortcomings, confessing that I was wholly unacquainted with the topography of the upper mountains, the streams that would have to be crossed, and the wild sheep-eating animals, etc.; in short that, what with bears, coyotes, rivers, canyons, and thorny, bewildering chaparral, I feared that half or more of his flock would be lost.

JOHN MUIR

"WILDCAT CASCADES," NEAR BERKELEY

A tiny pueblo founded by the Spanish in the late 18th century, Los Angeles—its Church of Our Lady the Queen of the Angels built 1818-1822—is one of the oldest settlements on America's West Coast . . .

California, the most spectacular and most diversified American state, California so ripe, golden, yeasty, churning in flux, is a world of its own in this trip we are beginning. It contains both the most sophisticated and the most bigoted community in America; it is a bursting cornucopia of peoples as well as of fruit, glaciers, sunshine, desert, and petroleum. There are several Californias, and the state is at once demented and very sane, adolescent and mature, depending on the point of view. Also, it is blessed by supernal wonders in the realm of climate, and a major item controlling its political behavior is the Pacific Ocean. The story of California is the story of migrations—migrations both into and within the state. The intense fluidity of America, its nomadism, is a factor never to be discounted.

JOHN GUNTHER

Inside U.S.A., 1947

SCENES IN LOS ANGELES

. . . yet one of its youngest and most vital—bursting out, amoeba-like in all directions, extending from the sea to the foot of coastal ranges—a melting pot for peoples of every continent and state

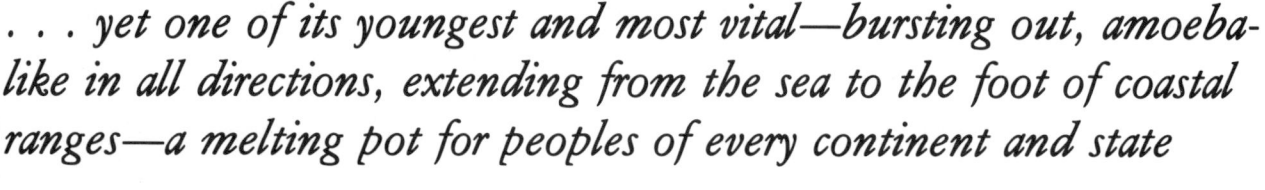

Los Angeles has been called every name in the book, from "nineteen suburbs in search of a metropolis" to a "circus without a tent" to "less a city than a perpetual convention." Frank Lloyd Wright, the architect, is supposed to have said once, "If you tilt the whole country sideways, Los Angeles is the place where everything loose will fall." And listen to Westbrook Pegler: "It is hereby earnestly proposed that the U.S.A. would be much better off if that big, sprawling, incoherent, shapeless, slobbering civic idiot in the family of American communities could be declared incompetent and placed in charge of a guardian like any individual mental defective." Freakishness, however, is not the characteristic that makes the town most interesting. What distinguishes it more is *(a)* its octopuslike growth, and *(b)* the way it lives on climate, mobility, and water . . . In general what is going on is a spreading out of the *city* of Los Angeles to a point where it will some day be coterminous with the county.

JOHN GUNTHER
Inside U.S.A., 1947

Father Junipero Serra started the chain of Franciscan missions—first building San Diego in 1769, Monterey in 1770, San Juan Capistrano in 1776—and is reputed to have planted the first California vineyard.

Of grapes, it is hardly yet time to speak so sanguinely as many do; for years will be required to render certain their exemption from the diseases and the devastators known to other lands of the vine. But it is certain that some kinds of grapes have been grown around the old Jesuit Missions for generations, with little care and much success; while it does not appear that the more delicate varieties recently introduced are less thrifty or more subject to attack than their Spanish predecessors, and vineyards are being multiplied and expanded in almost every farming neighborhood; single vines and patches of choice varieties are shooting up in almost every garden throughout the mining regions; and there can be little doubt that California is already better supplied with the grape than any other state of the Union. That she is destined soon to become largely and profitably engaged in the manufacture and exportation of wine is a current belief here, which I am at once unable and disinclined to controvert.   HORACE GREELEY

An Overland Journey, 1859

The mother vine, *vinta madre,* was also found at San Gabriel. To it the fathers had brought vine slips of a Spanish variety, known universally as the Mission grape. While these were growing, *aguardiente* was manufactured from the wild grapes of the country. In 1831 this pioneer vineyard contained 50,000 vines, and 50,000 more had been distributed along the Indian *rancherias.*   JOHN MUIR, ED.

Picturesque California, 1888

SANTA BARBARA AND VICINITY

1. City Hall and Hall of Records.   2. A Street.   3. Rose Cottage.   4. Roses in Private Grounds.   5. Ruin near the Mission.   6. The Beach and Bath-Houses. 7. In the Garden of the Mission.   8. The Old Mission.   9. Private Residence.   10. The Cliffs and Sea-Shore.

The Pacific Northwest

COLUMBIA RIVER . . . CAPE

HORN . . . MOUNT HOOD . . .ROOSTER

ROCK . . . PORTLAND . . . MOUTH OF

THE COLUMBIA . . . ASTORIA . . .

LOGGING AND LUMBERING SCENES . . .

TACOMA . . . PACIFIC AVENUE . . .

MOUNT TACOMA . . . THE WHARVES . . .

SEATTLE . . . SNOQUALMIE FALLS . . .

OLYMPIC MOUNTAINS . . .LAKE

WASHINGTON . . . MOUNT BAKER . . .

PUGET SOUND . . . SPOKANE FALLS . . .

RIVERSIDE AVENUE

COLUMBIA RIVER

The Pacific Northwest

THE PACIFIC NORTHWEST WAS America's "last frontier." Two centuries after New England saw its first permanent settlement, the Northwest still had only a few isolated fur-trading posts. It was not until late in the eighteenth century that Europeans took any interest in this land of mountains, rain forests, and fog-hung cliffs. Virtually unexplored beyond its rocky coast, it was known then only through rumor and myth.

In 1792 Robert Gray, captain of the American brig *Columbia,* entered and explored the mouth of the Columbia River and named it after his ship. His reports of the voyage served to end the centuries-old speculation about a Northwest passage. Late in 1805 Lewis and Clark reached the Pacific and wintered on the banks of the Columbia. Their detailed description of the topography, the resources, and the natives of the region west of the Continental Divide gave the West to Americans "as something their minds could deal with," in Bernard de Voto's words. This unknown and uncharted land finally became real, visible, and desirable. Within a few years it would become a land to settle in and, if necessary, to fight for.

The rich trade in the skins of sea otters first drew Europeans to the region. The Spanish had withdrawn their claims to the Northwest in 1793, and the British looked to be its heirs. The Northwest Company and the Hudson Bay Company were already actively engaged in fur trading, as was John Jacob Astor's Pacific Fur Trading Company. In 1812, at the start of the war with the British, Astor withdrew briefly from the territory, but reentered it after the war. The terms of the Treaty of Ghent, which ended the war, guaranteed joint British-American control of the region. But the growing American migration into the Northwest would shortly make this unworkable.

In 1840 the Reverend Jason Lee, who had lived in the the Northwest for some time, traveled east to petition Congress for a territorial government for Oregon. He then returned to Oregon with fifty-one settlers, who called themselves "The Great Enforcement." They settled in the Willamette Valley, south of the Columbia River. Lee's migration inaugurated the Great Migration that began in 1843. Thousands of pioneers traveled the Oregon Trail in covered wagons, suffering the intense heat of the desolate land east of the Cascade Range, and risking the winter hardships of the mountain crossing. They came in such large numbers that for a century after it was possible to follow their trail by the deep ruts cut by the wagon wheels.

The Great Migration of 1843 worried the British, who sent warships to the mouth of the Columbia. In 1844 James Polk was elected president on the platform "fifty-four forty or fight"—a slogan reflecting the extreme demand of the expansionists to extend American authority up to Russia's Alaskan holdings at 54.40 degrees north latitude. The question was settled peacefully; the British withdrew to the forty-ninth parallel, below Vancouver Island.

Congress and most Easterners then relaxed into indifference regarding the newly acquired land. It was still a long way away: over two thousand miles overland from the Midwest frontier or a sea voyage from New York or Boston that meant two or three years away

from home. The "Whitman Massacre" reawakened Congress and the public. In 1847 a Presbyterian missionary, Marcus Whitman, and his wife Narcissa, along with twelve others, were murdered by Cayuse Indians in the Walla Walla region of what is now Washington State. The provisional government then operating in the territory hunted down and executed the Indians, and dispatched a messenger to Washington to relate the news. They sent Joe Meek, a huge, buckskinned mountaineer, whose sensational appearance with news of the massacre stirred renewed interest in the Northwest. Within the year the region became a territory. Oregon and Washington were officially divided in 1853. In 1859 Oregon became the thirty-third state; in 1889 Washington became the forty-second state.

Most settlers made their way across eastern Washington and Oregon, over the Cascade Range, and into the heavily forested western region. East of the Cascades the land is desolate and brutally dry, but just at the crest of the mountains the climate suddenly changes, and the land to the west is some of the wettest in the nation. This is the land of the massive Douglas fir and Sitka spruce, trees that became the basis of the Northwest's economy for most of the century.

Despite the migration of the 1840s, the Northwest remained geographically and economically isolated for the next thirty years. In 1870 there were more people in the city of San Francisco than in all of Washington and Oregon. The region's isolation ended, however, with the arrival of the railroads in the 1880s. Between 1880 and 1890 the population of Oregon doubled and Washington's population grew fourfold. Tacoma, Seattle, and Portland thrived on lumber wealth, as rail connections to the East vastly expanded the market. Then, in 1897, the SS Portland docked in Seattle's harbor. It was reported that she carried a ton of solid gold found in Alaska. In fact, it was a ton of gold dust, found not in Alaska but in the Canadian Yukon. These details troubled no one. Americans, suffering a severe economic depression, reacted wildly to the news and the Gold Rush of '98 brought thousands to Washington's ports. The population swelled. America's "last frontier" became the jumping-off place for a journey into a new, harsher frontier—Alaska.

The vast Oregon Territory, extending to Washington and Idaho: rich in luxuriant forests, fertile soil, rivers abounding in salmon, and with notably large beaver colonies . . .

On the Olympic Peninsula in Washington, the wilderness stands unchanged since the first dawn. On the windward side of the mountains, 150 inches of rain will fall in an average year, and these primitive rainforests are rank and dark, full of wild beasts and twenty-foot ferns that grow in Pleistocene silence from the forest floor. The Olympic Mountains, a miniature Himalaya, rise sharp and snow-capped from the center of this low arboreal jungle. Saturated clouds obscure the peaks a good part of the year, casting a mood of Kieregaardian introspection over the entire massif. You could circle the peninsula for days on end and never know those mountains were there, yet sometimes they will stand out crisp and wild from the sea. . . . Now the Columbia is a commercial thoroughfare of vast international importance, and if you follow it upstream towards The Dalles, you will see its banks change before your eyes in a few minutes, from the lush, rain-blessed slopes of the windward side of the mountains to the sere plateau. It's like moving from the Garden into the desert wilderness.

CALVIN KENTFIELD

CAPE HORN

. . .attracted a flood of fur traders and pioneer-farmers, especially after the government-sponsored expeditions of John C. Fremont—the "pathfinder"—and his reports, in 1845

ROOSTER ROCK

Serene, indifferent of Fate,
Thou sittest at the Western Gate.

Upon the heights so lately won
Still slant the banners of the sun;
Thou seest the white seas strike their tents,
O Warder of two Continents!

And scornful of the peace that flies
Thy angry winds and sullen skies,
Thou drawest all things small or great
To thee, beside the Western Gate.

When forms familiar shall give place
To stranger speech and newer face;
When all her throes and anxious fears
Lie hushed in the repose of years;
When Art shall raise and Culture lift
The sensual joys and meaner thrift,
And all fulfilled the vision we
Who watch and wait shall never see,
Who in the morning of her race
Toiled fair or meanly in our place,
But, yielding to the common lot,
Lie unrecorded and forgot.

BRET HARTE

MOUNT HOOD

The cities of the Northwest burgeoned at a great rate—reflecting the wealth of coastal fisheries, valuable timber, and farmland yielding apples, pears, sugar beets, and truck vegetables . . .

First to define terms. It would seem that we have been in western regions a long time already, but actually in one sense California, Oregon, and Washington are not "the West" at all. In Portland I actually heard a lady say that she was "going West" on a brief trip—and she meant Utah! People on the Pacific Coast think of themselves as belonging to the "coast"; the "West" is quite something else again. Let us, however, be more inclusive. Of course the West comprises all the eleven states that lie wholly or in part west of the Continental Divide from any national point of view. But of these the three fronting the Pacific are a special case.

JOHN GUNTHER

Inside U.S.A., 1947

PORTLAND, OREGON

TILLAMOOK LIGHT.

VIEW OF ASTORIA.

SALMON FISHING NEAR PILLAR ROCK.

MOUTH OF THE COLUMBIA RIVER

In Paul Bunyan's Washington realm—truly the Evergreen State—were
millions of acres of Douglas fir, hemlock, ponderosa and sugar pine:
a land of Indian names—Skookumchuk, Dosewallips, and Puyallup

LOGGING SCENES—FROM FOREST TO RAFT

The most attractive sight which we had yet met with upon this voyage, now presented itself to our view. The steam-boat lay too close to the willow thicket, and we saw, immediately before us, the numerous, motley, gaily painted, and variously ornamented crowd of the most elegant Indians on the whole course. The handsomest and most robust persons, of both sexes and all ages, in highly original, graceful, and characteristic costumes, appeared, thronged together, to our astonished eye; and there was, all at once, so much to see and observe, that we anxiously profited by every moment to catch only the main features of this unique picture. . . All these Indians were dressed in their very finest clothes, and they completely attained their object; for they made, at least upon us strangers, a very lively impression. Many of them were distinguished by wearing leather shirts, of exquisite workmanship, which they obtain by barter from the Crows. Several tall, athletic men were on horseback, and managed their horses, which were frightened by the noise of the steam-boats, with an ease which afforded us pleasure.

MAXIMILIAN, PRINCE OF WIED

Travels in the Interior of North America, 1843

PUYALLUP HOP RANCH, TACOMA, WASHINGTON TERRITORY

John Muir observed: "The forests of America, however slighted by man, must have been a great delight to God, because they were the best He ever planted"

HAULING, SAWING, AND
FLOATING LOGS TO MARKET

Selective logging means simply that a "stand" of timber should not be cut down in sections willy-nilly, but that only mature trees should be chosen, and that enough growing trees should remain to bear seed and produce, in time, their successors. Such a process will, in the end, make for sustained yield, which means just what it says. It will keep the forests going, instead of destroying them; it will preserve this precious and indispensable natural resource, instead of throwing it away. The timber tycoons had a slogan once—"trees are a crop." As a matter of fact they are not. The only authentic crop from a tree is the cone. It takes a minimum of 80 years for a Douglas fir to reach sawlog size, from 140 to 180 for a ponderosa pine. So, in a sense, these trees do make a crop—every 80 to 180 years. But the lumber industry was based for a couple of generations on the philosophy of harvesting a "crop" that was not renewed. Timber was the first of the great beneficent American heritages. This country is unique—it still has virgin "old growth" timber that was here when the white man came. Almost everywhere else in the world, the virgin timber had disappeared by the time people got around to trying to manage it. We in the United States have actually been able to put virgin stands under management, but we have been very late to do so.   JOHN GUNTHER

Inside U.S.A., 1946

A century ago, the timber barons and their loggers—assuming the forests to be inexhaustible—cut great swaths of "old growth" acreage, before conservationists enforced selective logging

CUTTING AND TRANSPORTING LOGS TO MARKET

The loggers arrived in the Northwest still cherishing the idea they had held for nigh three hundred years: There was always timber, plenty of timber, just over the next hump. They had already cut a swath of it from eastern Maine through the lake states, and some had moved south to do as much for the timbered states bordering the Gulf of Mexico. The rest loaded their gear and themselves into the steam cars for Oregon and Washington. Loggers never looked backward, eastward. Had they done so, the more reflective among them might have seen what was happening—that as fast as they abandoned their old works a horde of farmers, traders, and city promoters moved in to grub stumps, plat towns, and make highways of the grass-grown logging roads. It was the loggers' ancient enemy, Civilization, following hard in their wake, and they wanted none of it. Yet here on the west coast, loggers and lumbermen were in their last stronghold, their backs to the sea. There was no hump to go over from here. Civilization had at last caught up with them; and it was going to tame them, too. Time out of mind their war cry had been to let daylight into the swamp, then to move on West. And now there was nothing west of the continent's west shore.

STEWARD HOLBROOK

The Romance of North America, 1958

Tacoma—at the head of navigation on Puget Sound, with two hundred miles of waterfront, built upon the prosperity of lumber reserves and sawmills—typifies the mushroom growth of Northwest frontier towns

Here is the city of Tacoma, one of the very latest creations of the modern pioneer. The peculiar advantages of its site have been known ever since Puget Sound was discovered, and yet the march of civilization would not be there now if the modern pioneer had not pushed it to the head of Commencement Bay and left it there. He could not very well have pushed it farther, because Tacoma is absolutely the last trench of the march of empire. In Tacoma there is no West. The pioneer in this case was the Northern Pacific Railroad. There came a time in the construction of this great steel throughfare when a definite limit had to be placed upon its westward progress—when some spot should be picked out and called the end of the road. The managers of the road picked out the head of Commencement Bay, and put it down on their maps as Tacoma, the western terminus of the Northern Pacific Railroad. There was a sort of sawmill community there at the time, but the able-bodied men in it would hardly have made a corporal's guard; and when it heard that it was to become one of the important cities of the American continent it simply gasped in awe and wonder. . . .

1. A Bit of Ninth Street.   2. Wheat Warehouses.   3. Pacific Avenue.   4. Elevator and Coal-Bunkers.   5. A View from Railroad Bridge.   6. Mount Tacoma, fro

TACOMA AND ENVIRONS

Majestic Mount Rainier dominates the scenic splendor of the environs—but more important are the hustle and bustle of this seaport: shipping wheat, lumber, canned fish, fruits, and vegetables

The soil that is favorable to the growing of hops is rich enough for almost anything else, which is fully shown in the variety and excellence of other things that thrive in the new State. The people assert that they can raise better fruit than California can, and more of it, with the exception of oranges and lemons and other tropical fruits. As the State is new and undeveloped, the agricultural possibilities are as yet hardly appreciated. The climate is unusually well adapted to fruit-culture, and, in fact, to the growing of all manner of grains, vegetables, and grasses. The winters are mild and equable, with a temperature like that of Tennessee. The summers are long and cool. In winter-time one would naturally expect at Tacoma the climate of the Arctic circle, but the geographical position is here at fault, at least so far as practical results are concerned. Were there no such thing as the warm current of Japan beating against the Pacific coast, the chief winter feature here would be the ice palace. As a result Tacoma has more rain than snow. Much of the rain in Tacoma is little more than a sort of Scotch mist and people get accustomed to that sort of thing in time.

Harper's Weekly, June 20, 1891

the Union Club.   7. Along the Wharves.   8. A Tacoma Saw-Mill.   9. A Typical Home.   10.   The oldest Bell Tower in America.   11. The Tacoma Theatre.

Seattle—a remote village with a handful of settlers, when founded in 1851; with a few thousand in 1880—soon expanded, as it became the gateway to the Northwest and distant Alaska . . .

The sounds that have influenced us in the Northwest are the crash of timber and the savage music of the whining head-saws on the sandspits of Puget Sound, on the banks of the Columbia, and elsewhere in the two states. The aroma that stirs us most is that of fresh saw-dust wild on the wind. Roughly sixty cents of every dollar in the region derives from forest products. There are two distinctive forests in the region. West of the Cascades is the forest dominated by the massive Douglas fir, with which is mixed hemlock, and where, in the coastal strip called the Rain Forest, stands the gigantic Sitka spruce. East of the Cascades are the immense timber stands of pine bordering the grasslands and deserts. Logging here was not of major importance until the arrival of the several transcontinental railroads. Rain is the great tree maker, and rain up to the extreme measure of 130 inches a year falls in the coastal region of the two states. At the summit of the Cascades, however, the moisture lessens markedly, and presently all but disappears. It is here that the Douglas fir forest begins to diminish and the pine takes over. This is the dividing line between two vastly different climates. It often divides the political thought of both states. Perhaps nowhere else in the United States is the transition from one climate to another so sharp and sudden as in the Cascade Mountain passes, including the Columbia River highway. Less than half an hour takes you from one to the other. The change can be felt and seen . . .

SEATTLE AND VICINITY ON PUGET SOUND

1. View of Seattle and Mount Tacoma from Hotel Denny.   2. Snoqualmie Falls, 286 Feet High.   3. Distant View of t

. . . Klondike gold fields boomed; Alaska's timber crop and fisheries flourished; steamship lines and trading companies developed; all home-based in progressive Seattle

. . . In contrast to the standard type of city boomer, talking shrill and fast of projected railroads, gaslights, and streetcars, the Puget Sound region attracted an extraordinary number of settlers who were seeking not the conventional metropolis, but the ideal community symbolized in the anagram of "nowhere" which Samuel Butler, an Englishman, used as title for his celebrated philosophical novel. *Erewhon* had no slums. It had no poor. It had a great deal of milk and no little honey. All hands lived on the sunny side of the street. Later and still more influential came a book called *Looking Backward*, by Edward Bellamy, an American, who also seemed to think the future of man lay in cooperative effort. Because the Northwest corner was a new region and not yet wholly corrupted by materialism, it seemed—in the eighties and nineties to thousands of Americans— that this was the place to establish the perfect Erewhon. So they came, the idealists, to found their Edens, under various names, mostly on the bays of Puget Sound and adjacent waters. There was the Puget Sound Colony, or Model Commonwealth, near present Port Angeles; the Glennis Socialists near Tacoma; the Co-operative Commonwealth of Equality, near Edison; the Cooperative Brotherhood of Burley; the Freeland Association on Whidby Island; and the Mutual Home Colony Association of Home, on Joe's Bay.

STEWART HOLBROOK

The Romance of North America, 1958

tains.   4. View of the City from the Bay.   5. Lake Washington.   6. View of Mount Baker.   7. On the Sound.

Spokane Falls—four hundred miles east of the Pacific, on the fringe of Washington Territory—grew from frontier hamlet to boom town, with valuable mines, horses and cattle, and luxuriant grazing land

It is the street of a town. It is quiet, almost as quiet as the woods, the hill crest, and the pond that can be reached in ten minutes from the center. The town has no vision of becoming a city. None of its inhabitants expects to become a millionaire. The basis of its vigor and its magnetism is quite simple and it is also quite real. One is freer here than elsewhere to be oneself. there are space, leisure, and freedom for personality to develop. One may follow his calling and raise his family in decent self-respect with less pressure to conform to the prepossessions or timidity of others, with more immunity from the dictation of fashion or belief or group passion or group orthodoxy.

BERNARD DE VOTO

The Romance of North America, 1958

Riverside Avenue

SPOKANE FALLS, WASHINGTON TERRITORY

No, the American dream that has lured tens of millions of all nations to our shores in the past century has not been a dream of merely material plenty, though that has doubtless counted heavily. It has been much more than that. It has been a dream of being able to grow to fullest development as man and woman, unhampered by the barriers which had slowly been erected in older civilizations, unrepressed by social orders which had developed for the benefit of classes rather than for the simple human being of any and every class. And that dream has been realized more fully in actual life here than anywhere else, though very imperfectly even among ourselves. It has been a great epic and a great dream.

JAMES TRUSLOW ADAMS

The Epic of America, 1933

Howard Street

List of Authors

Acknowledgments

Notes

Notes

Notes

Notes

Notes

Notes

Notes

Notes

Notes

Notes

Notes

Notes

Notes